We'll Meet Aga

All best wishes,

Patrick B. Hayes

July 2008.

By the same author:

Ghost Stories of Sutton Coldfield
Ghost Stories of Erdington

We'll Meet Again.

Edited by Patrick B Hayes.

Photography by Michael Madden.

Produced by Vera Green, Tilly Chapman, Deborah Shorey andEve Morris.

BREWIN
BOOKS

First published by Brewin Books Ltd
Studley, Warwickshire. B80 7LG
in December 2000

British Library Cataloguing In Publication Data.
A Catalogue record for this book is
available from the British Library.

ISBN 1 85858 172 9

Typeset in Palatino.
Made and printed in Great Britain by
SupaPrint (Redditch) Ltd

We'll Meet Again was produced by,

The Editorial Board:
Tilly Chapman, Joan Day, Vera Green, Deborah Shorey and Eve Morris.

The board would like to thank the following for all their help:

Community Groups:
Castle Vale Over Fifties Club, Mere Green Over Fifties Club, Falcon Lodge Derby & Joan, The Friends of Rookery House, and The Birmingham Jewish Ex-Service Association Men & Womens'

Individual contributors:
Lucien Baudon, Renée Brégent, Kenneth Bloor, Ted Essex, Frank Feld, Frank Flanner, Dorothy Fleming, Clare Hayes, Maurice Horton, Violet Horsley, Jean Marais, Janek Piela, Thomas Paine, Joe and Marjorie Ovadia.

"Backroom boys and girls."
Sally Potter, Theresa Tammam, Linda Kelly, Bob Brueton and Gavin Willets from Leisure Services, Birmingham City Council.

Bella Hamblin.
Vanessa Cusack at Quest Millennium.
Valerie Baudon, Sophie Bregent, Veronique Nonnenmacher and Anne Pichon.
Pat Spencer and Sue Fenoughty (Dig For Victory)
Alanna Dancey at Castle Vale Library.

Introduction.

This summer I was fortunate enough to go to France. My first night was spent in a camper van on Cap Gris Nez just outside Calais. I woke up around 9.00am to a beautiful view of headland and blue sea. My first morning in France, and it looked lovely. I walked around the old gun emplacements that lay on the headland. The old bunkers were spacious and looked like sturdy but empty shells. The guns had gone and they were silent now. This was the place where Reichsmarschall Herman Goring stood and watched droves of bombers from the Luftwaffe heading for London in 1940 when the blitz was about to begin.

I went inside and looked through the window where German soldiers once looked. There the English Channel or La Manche could be made out. Now, blue and calm with white coloured ferries steadily chugging across the sea.

I thought of those men who constantly looked across the waters to the cliffs of Dover. It is easy to see England, especially on a fine summer's day. I thought of that brave flotilla of boats that crossed the channel to Dunkirk during those dark days in June 1940.

I walked outside and noticed the grassy slopes with yellow flowers. A slight breeze blew in from the coast. I thought of the war as I sat on top of the old concrete bunker. I closed my eyes to soak up the morning sun and gentle breeze. After a few moments I could hear German voices. I then could hear the sound of a plane, the sound of a single propeller over head. I opened my eyes and next to me I saw two German tourists chatting and above a single engine plane humming through the sky. It could have been 1940! The cliffs of Dover were so near.

After a few moments I looked around to see three young people standing on the gun emplacements. There were two handsome young men and a pretty girl. They were blonde and wore white T-shirts. They spoke in German. It was such a poignant moment. Sixty years ago young German men fought young English men across Europe and Africa even on the seas of the Atlantic. Now what thoughts did these young people, standing in their T- Shirts and shorts have? Exam results? Football stars and dates? Our fathers fought your fathers was the thought that came to mind.

I looked again and they were gone. The breeze blew slightly stronger and the small flowers gave a shiver. The warm morning sun promised a lovely summer's day. The guns have gone now. The guns are silent now. Let's hope forever.

S. B. Hayes

CONTENTS

A Soldier's Life.

A soldier's life must be very hard
Especially as times are now
He must help for freedom
And to his country bow.

When he leaves home to go to the front
I wonder what he thinks in his heart
For all the loved ones he left behind
Must have been very hard to part.

But when out on the battlefield
With the smell of death around
He hasn't much time to think of home
Because the tyrant has to be found.

The battle must nearly drive him mad
When he hears the groans of the wounded
But he knows he must fight very hard
If victory is to be founded.

He must be sick of all the slaughter
And around him piles of dead
And as for playing a killers' role
I think he would rather be home instead.

And maybe when the war is over
And we've won victory
He'll come back to England
And forever more be free.

Linda Conroy. Castle Vale.

Linda wrote this poem during the war when she was seventeen years of
age. After writing it she put it in a teapot and only recently took it out to
read!

The first reminiscences that I recorded were told to me by the women from the Falcon Lodge Community Centre, Sutton Coldfield. Falcon Lodge is a post war housing estate that lies on the edge of Sutton Coldfield. On one side lies the Royal Town of Sutton Coldfield on the other side the wide, open fields of Warwickshire. During the war the RAF had been stationed at nearby Moxhull Hall and only a mile away the army was stationed at St George's Barracks.

The group I met were all women who had lived during the war and had many varied and different experiences to tell.

Tilly Chapman.

When the war started I was getting on for twenty years of age. I shall always remember if we had a bad air raid, because my mother used to call us in the morning and say, "Come on, you'll have to get up a bit early this morning as they were here again last night and you'll have a lot further to walk. The trams won't take you all the way."

You got so used to it that it just became a matter of fact. We had to get up and those were the things we had to do. It was a way of life and actually everyone seemed to pull together, everyone helped one another, was generous. They were bad years but in lots of ways they taught us a lot as well.

Doris Roberts.

There was a searchlight at Princess Alice's home on the Chester Road. We called it Big Bertha and one night a German plane got caught in Big Bertha and it dropped a salvo of bombs, one of which landed in our front garden, 316, Jockey Road.

We were all in bed and Father came to get us out. He had to get Mother by the head and tip her upside down as the lintel window was only two inches away from her. Father pulled her out, turned her over and pulled the rubble off her. We scrambled down the stairs and Dad was standing by the front door and he shouted, "You can't go that far."

We made our way to the shelter only to find our next door's neighbours were in the shelter first. Dad never used to go to the shelter, which was in the back garden. It had bedding and food down there as you got ready for a siege.

My neighbour was in first, she had the best part and we all had to pile in after her. Our loo was upstairs in the house and had been flattened as the bomb had taken the front of the house off.

So we all got into the shelter and then Mother said that she wanted to go to the toilet. We asked Mrs Street, who lived next door, if we could use her toilet and she said, "No, no, you can't come to mine."

I think she was frightened, you see, so Mother went in the garden. It was really funny as Dad came round and said, "Are you all, all right in there?" "Yes," we replied and Mother said, "And you'd be better off if you put your trousers on." He had been walking around without any trousers on. It was a real experience!

The back of the house was still unstable, so us girls had to be farmed out to neighbours. Looking back, my Mother was very lucky that night.

DUNLOP DAYS.

I was working in the buffet in Commercial Offices, serving the dinners and snacks. The sirens would go and the place would empty and we were allowed to take what we liked in our pockets. We would then go and sit on the stairs in the middle of the building and munch our stuff. We were allowed to take exactly what we wanted.

Olive Brownlee.

I wasn't in Coventry for the November blitz but I was there for the April Blitz. I had been in Birmingham previously and I thought that was hor-rific enough, but Coventry that was just devastation, there was no other word for it. You went into a shelter and when you came out all you saw, all around you was ruins, nothing else, whole streets were down. There were fires burning and there were people searching around for relatives and looking for anyone else they might know. I don't think I ever lived or will live to see anything so terrible as that April blitz.

Being in the shelter, we knew by the crunch of the bombs as they came down, it was bad but we didn't realise until the next morning when the Air Raid Warden got us out it would be as bad as it was. All the shops, there was nothing left of them, all the stuff lying in the streets. It was just horrible, the whole thing was horrible and when you looked round there was nothing left standing.

We moved back to Smethwick. My brother and I would not go to the shelter at night because there were always arguments, and rows in the family. We would just not go. One night Mom was in the shelter and my dad was in his usual spot outside the back door, because he wouldn't go down either. We heard this plane coming down and my brother rushed into my bedroom and said, "It's going to crash, Olive, it's going to crash."

I replied, "There's nothing we can do about it."
The next thing we knew there was this great orange flame, which shot up into the air. Of course we were down stairs quicker than you could have said, "Night". We grabbed some clothes and ran off. My Father said, "You'll stay here, you 'll stay here."

"No" we replied, " we're going to see where it is." We ran outside.
In those days we lived on Warley Road but it has been renamed Thimblemill Road now. We ran up the hill and there was this plane and it had hit a house. We didn't know till later that the girl who lived in this house was killed. She'd been due to be married the next day. Well, they got the pilot and another one out but if the police hadn't arrived they would have been killed, would have been pulled to pieces by the people who lived around there. It was terrible. The plane still had bombs on and they were busy trying to get us away in case more tragedy happened. But everyone was so angry; it was a horrific sight.

I used to work in Birmingham and I was there one night when it was bombed. The year was 1940. When the sirens went you had to get off the streets. You couldn't stay on the streets. We were at Marshal and Snelgrove, on New Street. I liked to go there for a cup of tea and a sandwich. Also, my Mom and Dad would know where I was.

They used to say you never heard the bomb that hit you. Well, we could hear these damn bombs coming down all around us. So we went down to the shelters underneath the store. The bombing stopped about at 2.00 in the morning. The All Clear hadn't gone but the Air Raid Warden came down and said, "I'm sorry but we have to get you out. We've got to get you out."

I thought, "Oh my God, what's happening now?"

When we surfaced we could not believe it. There were flames everywhere. I thought I would walk as far as the Hall of Memory and hopefully I would see some one I knew. We were only allowed to go as far as Broad Street.

I always remember I had a white coat on but when I got to the top of Broad Street it was a pale black! They weren't letting anything into Birmingham only the beer lorries. You walked along the street, the gold was running down the road from the Jeweller's shop and there were fur coats lying everywhere! When I got up to the top of Broad Street a policeman said to me, "Where do you think you're going?"

I replied, "I'm trying to walk home. I've had enough of this."

Meanwhile my Dad had walked from Smethwick all the way to Broad Street, as he knew what was happening. I saw my Dad before he saw me. We walked home together. On the way he said,

"You give that job up tomorrow. You're not going there again."

I never went back to Marshall and Snelgrove, as they had to pull it down. It received two or three direct hits. It got hit that night when we were in it!

Summer Holiday by Tilly Chapman.

I was on holiday in Teignmouth, with my husband Stan. When we got there, there was all this wire netting so we couldn't get right down to the beach. You could only go so far. This one-day, we were sitting on this wall near the sand. My husband was sitting beside me and I said, "It's lovely isn't it, Sitting here in the sunshine?"

Then all of a sudden we heard this groaning and we looked up and he said, "Oh my God,"

"What's the matter?" I said. I looked up and saw the planes and said, "Whose are those?"

"They're not ours, love," came the reply. We saw the planes flying just above the water. There we were sat as they flew towards us.

"Get your self down," Stan said. I don't know what I thought I was doing. I knelt and put my head down. When they had gone over he looked up and began laughing. He looked at me and said, "What caper were you getting up to?"

I said, "What you on about?"

"Your bum was sticking out! You were giving them a bloody good target!" he said.

When we got back to the hotel, we went upstairs to our bedroom we noticed that bullets had gone through the wall. A lot of the hotel was damaged and the wine and beer was running out of the bar. We all had to help by picking up the slabs from one of the damaged inside walls and chucking it through one of the windows. I always remember, the holidaymakers were actually going home as they did not wish to stay any longer.

Stan and I carried on clearing the big lounge at the top of the hotel. I said, "We better throw these pieces through the window."

I picked this big lump up and threw it out of the window. After a while he said, "You don't half pick your timing." He said.

"Why's that?" I replied.

"That poor old dear has gone up the hill quicker now than she did before. She must have thought there was another one of them behind her."

Apparently, an old lady was walking up the hill by the hotel. The sound of the rubble being thrown out of the window scared her so much she thought bombs were dropping so she ran up the hill as fast as she could. You had the funny side of the war as well. I never wrote and told my Mother what happened that day otherwise she would have had us on the next train home.

Doris Smith was in the Land Army. Up to 80,000 women joined the Land Army in order to increase agricultural production. Not only did they cultivate and harvest the land but also several thousands of them worked in the Timber Corps and some even worked as rat catchers!

Doris Smith, Land Army Girl.

I worked on a farm during in the war in Sutton Coldfield. I remember one-day I was harrowing in one of the fields after the digger had dug the potatoes up. We were right at the top of the field, at High Heath. It was quite a slope to come down. I was on the back of this horse and I heard a noise. I looked up and there in the sky was a dogfight-taking place. The noise of the machineguns must have frightened the horse because it bolted and there I was hanging on for grim death! The horse galloped all the way to the farmhouse. When he got home he stopped because he knew he was home.

Sheila Standley.

When the war was on and when the trams were running, everything had to be blacked out to stop the aeroplanes following the lights. I remember as a child being on the tram, all the windows were blacked out and you couldn't see where you were going. You had to count the stops, remember the stops and the name of each road so that you knew where you had to get off and it was just all black, really black.

One night our Mom and Dad had gone to fetch the groceries and a raid started. Our Joy who was looking after us, said, "You kids, get under the table." She pushed us three kids under the table. She was there as well but with half her bum sticking out! The bombs began to fall. Joy said, "This one is for us, so let's go down the cellar."

But our brother said, "No, if we go down the cellar we'll get gassed or the water pipe will burst."

So we didn't and stayed under the table. A bomb actually fell outside the house and it made a big crater in Birchfield Road where the trams came down. The hole was ever so big; I wouldn't like to think how big it was. I was more worried about the velvet dress that our Mom had got me, that I had left on the chair!

My sister and I weren't very old at the start of the war. We were a young family. I remember the Christmas of 1942. We had trimmed the entire house up with decorations and we were going to have goose for dinner. My elder sister had got married in the March; she was nineteen years old. I remember my brother-in-law saying to my Mom, "Save us a leg of the turkey." As he wasn't going to be there.

She said, "No, I won't, as we're having goose."

Anyway, Mom cooked this goose and we were all in a festive mood. At twelve o'clock dinnertime, there came a knock at the door. Dad answered the door and there was a policeman standing there. Mary my sister was standing at the back of the house. He said, "Is Mrs Barber here?" My Dad said, " Why? What do you want."

"I want to tell her some bad news."

"Can't it wait until tomorrow?" Dad asked.

"No" the constable stated.

"Well can't you tell me what you have to say?" Dad said.

"Well, her husband Frederick Barber has been fatally injured."

The policeman was standing on the steps and Dad was standing in the hallway.
My sister had only half heard what the policeman had said, but Dad came back in and said to my sister, "Fred won't be home because he has been injured."

"What do you mean injured? What hospital is he in?" My sister quizzed.

Dad thought he would keep the truth from her until Boxing Day and break it to her properly. My sister, being what she was, insisted on knowing what had happened to her husband.

She went to Lozells Road Police Station where Sergeant Pitt was the man in charge.

"I've come to see what's the matter with my husband. I've only been married nine months, I've been told he has been injured and I want to know what hospital he is in."

The policeman replied rather sharply, "Don't you know what fatally injured means, my dear?"

"What do you mean fatal?"

"Fatal means fatal. He's dead"

He died on Christmas day. He had been killed transporting a gun on the Towcester Road. The lorry had hit an ice patch and turned over. There were ten of them in the lorry and my sister's husband was the only married man amongst them. He was twenty-four. She was nineteen.

I have never seen trimmings come down as quick. We didn't have any goose. Christmas was over for us.

Frederick John Barber was buried at Witton cemetery on New Year's Eve. All the lads that were with him in the accident carried the coffin.

My sister never got over Fred. He was like a brother to me. I remember playing skipping with him in the garden. Once he blacked my Dad's shoes. He polished one but left the other.

"What I am supposed to do with this!" Dad shouted.

"I'll do the other one when I come back on leave." Fred laughed.

My other sister lost her boyfriend on D-Day. He was only 21.

Mary Sanders.

I used to live in an ordinary country Yorkshire village during the war. York was our nearest town. The Germans wanted to bomb the Rowntrees factory. They followed the river but one night they missed the river and they hit York Minster. All the buses were stopped; in fact everything stopped so that the bomb damage could be cleared up. There wasn't a great deal of damage but the nave was hit.

I lived in a village 10 miles outside York and it was in the middle of three aerodromes, Marston Moor, Lynton and Dishford. They were home to heavy bombers. We used to hear the bombers go over from Marston Moor. They would go over our village, over our houses. We would count them as they went out and we would count them coming back. We always knew if there was one missing.

Marston was a fairly big camp and it was about five miles away. The airmen used to come to our village and go to the Hammerton Hotel for a drink, as there wasn't a pub at Marston. There was also the army that was billeted at Hammerton Hall. That's where the officers stayed. The soldiers stayed in the lodge of the hall, which was two doors away from my parents. Also, there were Nissen huts in the fields full of soldiers and lorries. That's where I met my husband.

Mary Sanders from Yorkshire with daughter Jean.

There were also evacuees from London. We took in two girls. The mother also came; she had seven children in all! We could only take in two as we only had one spare bedroom. The mother lived next door with two of her children.

I remember all the soldiers getting ready for the Second Front.
Mine was a different kind of war, as we didn't get the bombings. We had a big garden, lots of fruit and vegetables, a hundred poultry and a pig. But of course all the boys went off to the war.

There was one boy from the village who didn't come back. His name was Ted Lumley. He went over to train as a pilot in Canada but he never came back. I think he died in an accident.

My cousin drove a tank and coming back from Dunkirk the tank rolled over and smashed his leg. The war was over for him as he spent most of his time in hospital.

I came down to Birmingham and I realised I had been in a different war.

Joan Glew.

I worked at the Seven Hours Cleaners on the Parade in Sutton Coldfield. We had a lot of Americans come in for their clothes to be cleaned. Officers would come in carrying batons and ask if they could have their clothes dry- cleaned quickly.

We had a lot of coloured and white Americans come in. The coloured Americans were always very, very polite, so were the white Americans but they were always a bit boastful as they had everything we didn't. We used to joke about it. The coloured Americans said they liked England because they were treated as equals and they enjoyed being here.

I never saw any racial discrimination; we treated them as anyone else. They were there for quite a while and it was good.

Vera Green.

I had three brothers; the youngest, Frank, went to India where he remained with the R.A.F for the duration. Tom was the next one and Jim was the eldest. Our surname was Langley.

Tom came back from Dunkirk and they sent him up to Scotland to recuperate and in the meantime, my older brother Jim had joined the army. At that time you could ask for a brother to be with you for the rest of the war. Anyway it was all planned and Tom was sent down and they went off to Crete together. As soon as they landed in Crete they were taken Prisoners of War. During that time every lunchtime of a Sunday, my mum would put the dinner on the table and my father would sit and cry. We would ask him why he was crying and he used to think that they, my brothers, hadn't got any food to eat. He didn't want his dinner, and this happened every Sunday throughout the war.

It would have been about 1941, Tom would have been about twenty-five and Jim was almost thirty. They were in the Engineers; they didn't see much of the war at all. We had letters and cards and we used to send them parcels and we had quite a bit of communication from them. They seemed to be all right when they came back. They never ever talked about it, never talked about the war at all; we asked questions but they wouldn't say anything. We don't really know what happened. The post must have come through the Red Cross. They used to send Christmas cards and all that sort of thing.

I met my husband when I started work when I was fourteen. His name was Leonard Bell. He was in the same workshop as me and we were apprentice tailors. We started courting and we had a tandem and we used to cycle down to Weston Super Mare and the Malverns. We used to start early in the evening, we used to cycle through the dark, and when we got to Weston, there used to be a cycling place, like the YMCA. We used to go there for the night and then the manager used to come and she would say, 'Boys downstairs at the back, girls upstairs at the front. And I don't want you coming down stairs in the night either.' She kept an eye on us. She was great. We used to go there quite often. Sometimes we used to go in a group, perhaps half a dozen of us and sometimes we would go on our own. It would take about six hours. It's amazing what you can do when you are young! It was marvellous really. It was great, I kept the bike after the war started I kept it for quite a long time. In Weston we would just look at the shops and play on the beach, all sorts of things. We only used to stay one night, as we had to go to work on the Monday.

Then the war came and Len was called up. He went with the first lot in July. He went on my birthday of course! He went into the Royal Artillery. The first day of his very first leave Len ended up in hospital. The army ambulance came to our house and he was taken to the Queen Elizabeth Hospital with appendicitis. Afterwards he was sent to recuperate near Tamworth. When going out he had to wear a bright blue suit, white shirt and a red tie. We were married before he rejoined his regiment.

On his next leave we went to see his friend's wife who lived with her family in Camden Street, near Spring Hill, Birmingham. While we were there we had a terrific raid. We were making tea for everyone when there was a big bang. When we went to look, Bulpitts factory across the road had been hit. The army and the firemen were there. The gutters were just rivers of fire.

After the raid was over we decided to go home. We had to walk to Sutton Coldfield. No trams, no buses. As we walked under the Railway Bridge in Farm Street, a soldier shouted, 'Who goes there?' We had to stop. After a short while he let us carry on our journey.

Before we got to Sutton Coldfield, we got to the top of Gravelly Hill. We stopped and looked back. It looked as if the whole of Birmingham was on fire. We got home in the early hours, thankful to be in one piece.

Len was mostly stationed around Kent and I used to get 36 hours pass to see him. The army would tell you when you could go and when to leave. We had great fun going to the concert parties.

I didn't think Len would go out of the country, it was now 1944 just after the D-Day Landings. His regiment, the 94th Field Regiment Royal Artillery landed in France near Caen. Soon afterwards, I received a letter to tell me to say that he had been killed on the 3rd of August. I knew that was impossible, because my cousin's husband met him over there on the 3rd of August. We were sending letters to one another and my cousin told me that he had met Len in France. So I knew that he couldn't have been killed on the 3rd of August, so I wrote back to the War Office. I had a letter back to say that Len had been out laying communication cables. He was hit by a mortar shell and died of his wounds, August 7th 1944. He was 26 years old.

The love I had. My eldest daughter was four and a half and I was expecting my second one and she was born three months after Len was killed.

The morning I got the letter to say that he was dead. I was living at home with mum and it didn't register at all and I just showed the letter to my mum and I think she reacted more than I did. I remember that she disappeared and I couldn't find her anywhere and my Grandma lived two doors away and my Aunt next door, so I thought she had gone there. I went around and she was at my grandmother's. She was worse than I was. We had to tell people that he had died. We had to go all the way to Kings Heath to his parents and they were out when we got there. We left a note on the door and later they came over to see us.

I didn't believe that he was really dead and I thought that one-day I was going to meet him again. I went with my dad to the Yenton pub. When we were in there the door opened and I looked up and this man walked in and he looked just like Len. Just the same, but slightly shorter. It turned out that he was an American soldier. It did upset me that did. I spoke to him, as my Dad knew all of them in there.
I think Dad missed my brothers so much that when he went to the pub for a drink, he would bring American and English soldiers back home and those stationed near our home used to call and see us.

I remember when my eldest daughter was born in 1941, because she was born at home at three minutes to twelve on a Saturday night. All the soldiers were outside sitting on the wall. One American soldier called Francis used to take her out in the pram.

I remember when the war was over, someone in our road made a life size dummy of Hitler and strung it up from the bedroom windows either side of the road. They then lit a fire underneath. My mother's piano was taken into the street and there was singing and dancing into the early hours.

During the summer when travelling through Normandy in France I thought of Vera's husband, Len. We passed a Military cemetery with its countless rows of crosses. I thought of the time when Vera and Len cycled through the night to Weston when all of England was asleep. They were two happy teenagers who saw life as an adventure. I guess that not for one moment did Len ever think as he cycled down the country lanes, that he would lose his life on the fields of France.

Captain D.E. Clarke Commanding Officer of Leonard Bell, pictured with his wife, Mrs Clarke.

Capt. D.K. Clarke, R.A.,
210/91 1st Regiment R.A.
I.B.A

21st October, 1944.

Dear Mrs. Bell,

Reference to your husbands death.

    I purposely did not write as the Padre told me
he'd written and I did not want to upset you. The exact
circumstances of his death were as follows:-

    We had a bad and very hard afternoon making an
attack and had been shelled heavily and Tinkle, as we
affectionately called him, had already got a splinter in his
tin helmet. During the evening things got quiet-r and at
11.15.p.m. I was ordered to report back with my crew to
Infantry Battalion H.Q.

    The four of use were 1st to climb into the truck
when a small 5 cm Morton launch burst in amongst us.
Tinkle was hit in the stomach and leg. The three of us
tied him up and I gave him a Morphia Tablet. These were
on the spot, some stretcher bearers came and he was taken
straight to the M.O. I myself called on the M.O. 45 minutes
later and learnt that Tinkle had been evacuated rearwards
immediately as a priority case. The M.O. told me that
there was just a 50/50 change of his pulling through if
he could get to the operating table within 6 hours.
I spoke to the infantry Padre who was just back the next
day and asked him to let me know the news of Tinkle.
When I saw him he told me he had died in the Ambulance.

    You probably realise that stomach wounds are
tricky things and everything possible was done for him.

    I want to tell you how much I miss Tinkle
who was my operator. He was extremely competent at his
job. Very brave and a really excellent companion.
He and I were in 2 or 3 very sticky shaves together
when we worked with tanks and I never want to work with
a better man.

    He was always talking about his house and his
daughter and of course the coming event. I miss him very
much as he was a frequent companion and
I should like to take this opportunity to condole with you
on your great loss. Words I'm afraid don't help much
but if there's anything I can do for you in any way
you have only got to let me know. Please accept once again
my sincerest sympathy.

                    Sincerely yours,

                    Dennis Clarke.

Letter from Captain Clarke explaining how Leonard "Tinkle" Bell died.

Kenneth Bloor resident of Erdington, Birmingham.

I joined the army in Birmingham and did my initial training at Ascot Racecourse where we had a camp.

I then went to France. I remember travelling across the country in a train for a terrific long time. We moved about a lot but didn't see any action until we were pushed back to Dunkirk, and we had no armaments at all, we had nothing. The Germans started pushing across France. They were pushing so fast we had to make our way back to England. We were walking for days before we got to the beach. A man on a motorbike kept telling us to move on down the beach. We were picked up by a Great Western Railway boat and taken back to England. When we got home we were on the defensive as the Germans were supposed to be following and were going to land. When we came back from France after Dunkirk we were always promised that as we were the last ones out of France we would be the first to return. I was a tank driver. It was difficult to learn at first, but soon I was able to move it around like a spinning top.

We did our tank training in Yorkshire on the moors and then all over England. Before D-Day we drove the tanks down to Dorset. Before we set sail for France we spent three days on the boat with the sailors. D-Day had been postponed because of the weather. When we were going over on the boat it was quite a nice sailing. We had our D-Day rations. Everything was in cubes; even tea was in cubes. The meals were all ready for you; all you had to do was pour hot water over it. There was dried milk and biscuits. Some of the things were very good actually, like the tinned soup.

When we got near the French coast we all stood up on top deck. There were boats coming towards us, there were shells coming from the Royal Navy ships and planes flew all over the place.

There were boats being blown up out of the water and the diesel oil caught fire. On our right there was a ship sending up rockets. I thought some thing had blown up the first time I saw it. There were these rockets going through the air like a ball of fire and we watched them land. They were aiming for the pillboxes and big guns.

Our tanks were American and they had to be waterproofed before the D-Day landings. They were waterproofed up to five feet so that when we came off the landing craft they would be able to carry on through the water and hopefully, onto the beach. It was six o'clock in the morning when I landed and the fighting had been going for a couple of hours. There were planes; battleships and you could hear the shells going over-head. We landed in two feet of water, there were lots of ships around us blown up and a quite a few of the tanks never made it. A lot of the sol-diers that landed went back on the same ship they came in, as they were wounded.

As we landed, there were tanks and infantry in front. I saw one infantry-man with a radio on his back. He had just been shot.

We landed on the beach in about two feet of water, and afterwards we made our way through Belgium and then crossed the Rhine, into Germany. The engineers had to build a bridge and then we drove over in our tanks. We didn't sleep in tents but in barns or hay ricks, anywhere that we could find. Some lads did sleep under their tanks but then we were issued with a warning. On no circumstances were we to sleep under our tanks. Some of the lads had been crushed as the tank had sunk into the ground during the night and no one could get them out. We used to sleep in holes and put camouflage over them. Mosquitoes plagued us, as they liked the night air. We soaked the netting in petrol to keep the mosquitoes away. One night one of the lads lit a cigarette and the whole netting went up. It was as if an explosion had gone up in the trench. Luckily, no one was hurt, only singed.

When we were in Germany we had to go into houses, but you had to be careful because as the Germans vacated the houses they would plant bombs. They would be attached to wires and they would go off when you opened a cupboard and sometimes they were attached to suitcases. A lot of that went on.

Leaflets were dropped written in German and those that wanted to sur-render only had to walk over to our lines and they would be given safe conduct. The leaflet showed the Germans how we had them surrounded.

After the war a rumour went round that Hitler hadn't died in the bunker but was really on the run. I've got some actual pictures of German sol-diers. I took them off a dead German. They never carried any valuables. After a battle we had to go through their pockets to find out who they were. I never found any gold rings though. They were in the infantry and our tanks had killed them.

After the training I went through I didn't feel anything. I found one German sitting up in a trench. A bullet had hit him right between the eyes, gone through his head and come out the other side, leaving a big hole.

On one occasion, we were in action and shells were actually landing in the field around us. I managed to take shelter in a square brick water butt, but I was lucky, it was empty at the time. Some of the crew from our tank dug a hole. Two of them dug this hole and a German shell landed in the middle and killed them outright. The Regimental Priest, the Padre came round and gave them the last rites and nearly fainted at the sight, when he saw them. We filled them in there and then in the hole. I heard later that the villagers kept it as a shrine and put chains around it. This was Overloon in Holland.

When we were in Germany we came across this farmhouse. There were a group of German farm workers sitting down having dinner. We had advanced so fast they didn't have time to leave. They were sitting down and having their meal and when we stormed in they immediately stood up and began singing the German National Anthem. One of them was playing the tune on the piano so my mate went up and smashed the piano with a sledgehammer!

We were in action one day and we were told that there were Germans in the area. My mate saw a pair of hands coming over the wall. He went up quietly and stuck his bayonet through one of the hands. It was a German soldier.

There was another time when there was some shelling going on and we came across a couple of Germans that had got killed in the shelling. We rounded the villagers up and got them to dig a hole. We thought it was funny, as there were now two less Germans.

Later on I was on sentry duty at a Displacements Persons Unit. I have a photograph of me inspecting a Russian soldier's papers. That was in Paddaborne in Germany. We still had to be cautious after the war, as there were so many land mines around.

After the war I made friends with a German family. When I say family there were only women and young children left. The mother of the family was telling me that her husband was in a big battle and that she had never heard of him since. I told her, "You won't see him again." She never heard what happened to him.

Kenneth Bloor was part of Operation Overlord. Overlord was the code name for the invasion of France, which took place on the 6th June 1944 in Normandy. The first wave of allied troops came on the beaches just after dawn. 57,000 US, 75,000 British and Canadian troops landed on the sands of northern France. The Americans met the most resistance on Omaha beach. For those who have seen the film, Private Ryan, they will be well aware of the horrors that befell the men. After the long day of battle it was possible to walk over the dead GIs from the shore to the headland without touching the sand.

After six weeks of heavy fighting the Allies were able to trap and capture 50,000 Germans before continuing eastwards. The fierce fighting brought casualties. An American cousin of mine, Frank Finnarty was killed after three days in France. He came from New York and was about to become a professional singer. They said he was as good as Bing Crosby and could even have been as famous as Sinatra. As with the potential of so many young men, it was wiped out in a second by a bullet or piece of shrapnel.

Kenneth Bloor (right) with Russian soldier in Germany at the end of the war.

Photograph of young German soldiers found by Kenneth Bloor.

Ted Essex resident of Walmley Sutton Coldfield.

There was a second parliament at Watford Gap, which is now near the motorway. This goes back to World War one. There is a complete parliamentary building there where the government could be evacuated. There are ventilation shafts for the railway. There is a canal link and a railway link too. You can see the aerials of the building from the road.

My father was with the Ministry of Defence during the war and if we ever went to Watford gap I would have to get out of the car whilst he drove through five miles of security checks. I have never found out to this day what went on. It was real, "Hush, hush."

Back in Sutton Coldfield we used to collect for the war effort. We used to collect aluminium for spitfires, loads of cast iron. We collected for H.M.S. Birmingham putting sixpence a week on a savings stamp. We hated Hitler's guts, but as children we loved the war.

There used to be a copse at the back of East View Road. When I was about nine years of age I went there with a group of friends. I was climbing this tree when some one yelled up at me. I came tumbling down and there was this man standing there wearing a mac.

"Who are you? What have you been doing?" He asked. "You've been over the farm over the road haven't you?"

The farm was the name for the place where the Home Guard kept their ammunition.

"No we haven't," I retorted.

"What do you mean, 'we', " he replied.

"Me and I my friends," I boldly stated.

Before he could reply one of my friends shouted, "Right lads, get him!"

Within seconds all six of us had him pinned on the ground.

"I'm a policeman, I'm a policeman," he shouted.

We loosened our grip and he pulled out his card. He was a Special Constable.

We thought he was a spy because he had been asking questions. He didn't look British and he was wearing a raincoat!

Once there was a raid and we saw a German plane being shot down. It was a Junker 88. As it crashed we noticed that it had dropped a load of incendiary bombs by the railway line. After the raid four us went out looking for shrapnel. We found some hexagon shaped things and took four of them to school and showed them to Nobby Harris our schoolmaster. We had posters up in school of all the anti-personal bombs and they didn't look anything like them.

"Please Mr Harris, what are these?" we asked innocently.

He sent us to the school's air raid shelter whilst he dealt with the problem! We had only brought in four live incendiary bombs!

There was another incident when a policeman stopped me for carrying a musket down Sutton High Street.

Maurice Horton resident of Walmley, Sutton Coldfield.

What happened in Sutton Park during the war? The Luftwaffe used to come over the East Coast and into the Midlands. They used the pools in the park as navigation points as they came in from the Northeast, which gave them directions to Coventry.

The authorities thought it would be a good idea to put a searchlight in the park. Unfortunately, guns didn't accompany the searchlight. It didn't take the Germans long to discover that there weren't any guns. I believe that the searchlight was somewhere between Coppice and the Jamboree Stone in the park. It was in a high position and was in the centre of all the pools. There is a memorial to the men in the park.

From what my Mother told me, on the nights of August the 8th and 9th when they were hitting Coventry they sent over a night fighter to precede the bombers. As normal they threw the searchlight up to try and thwart the fighter plane from picking up the pools in the park. However, what happened instead was that the fighter plane flew down the beam of the searchlight and shot everyone to pieces. Three men died and my Uncle Ted was one of them. All three of them are now buried in the military section of Witton cemetery side by side. One of them was Lieutenant Hood of the Royal Warwickshire Regiment, 47 years old, and the other one was Private H.W. Hill, Royal Army Service Army Corps. He was the driver. Then there was my Uncle, Private Edward Rushton from the 45th Searchlight Battery, Royal Artillery, lately of the Royal Warwickshire Regiment. He died from wounds in Sutton Cottage hospital, August 14th 1940. He left a widow, Lillian, and one child called June.

Almost next to Uncle Ted's grave is my cousin's. He was also killed in action. He was a Flight Sergeant and his name was Godfrey. He was actually killed on a bombing mission. He was getting married the week after and he had asked my Mom to buy him some white gloves he could wear at the wedding. Whether he was shot up during the raid or when the plane crashed when coming into landing I am not sure.

I had another Uncle who ended up burying the bodies in Belson with a bulldozer. His name was Albert. He was a tank driver and had had two tanks shot out from under him, so he volunteered for what he thought was a cushy job. Some job!

St George's down the road was an R.A.F. base and they had a go at that. They blew up 39 and 41 Whitehouse Common Road. I still have gaps in my wall, 2 inches wide, which have never being repaired! There was a man called Len Philpots who used to live in Whitehouse Common and he was a Spitfire pilot based at Castle Bromwich. He had a handle barred moustache and used to fly over the top of his house and he would fly very low almost touching the chimney pots. This meant he would "Buzz" his Mother, to let her know he was coming home for dinner!

I also knew a man called Harry Pope. He owned a butcher's shop on Kingsbury Road. He was my best friend's dad and he was called up during the war. He joined the R.A.F. and became a Flight Sergeant. He had a whole pile of aircraft that officially did not exist. He had rebuilt planes from the old smashed up ones. He had aircraft lined up, Lancasters, everything. The numbers did not officially exist as there were no logbooks and at the end of the war in Lincolnshire they dug a huge ditch and put the planes in it and officially to this day they do not exist. The aircraft were aircraft that had been badly damaged and thought to be un-repairable. When planes came in to be repaired the ones thought originally to be un-repairable went out with the other planes' logbooks!

There was also an Italian prisoner of war camp in Sutton. The prisoners would be sent out to the local farms and I heard that on one occasion there were some prisoners who were working on the drains. They installed the drains but filled them with bricks. They had to be called back to clear all the drains out and when they were asked why they filled the drains with bricks they said it was because they did not want to help the enemy.

Also in Sutton, it was the only place in the country where women belonged to the Home Guard. Sutton Park in 1944 was home to thousands of soldiers from all nationalities. It was one massive garrison. Canadians, Poles, Australians, Americans, every nationality and of course they used to visit all the local pubs! As a youngster I used to see the Americans walking down the street. I would say to them, "Got any gum chum?" and they would reply, "Yeah. Have you got a sister?"

"Yeah," I replied, "But she's only 12 years old!"

"That's no good, son." And they would walk off but they did give us the gum.

Private Edward Rushton, Royal Warks, who manned the searchlight that fateful night and later died from his wounds.

Reminisces from Castle Vale Over 50's group, Erdington.

Castle Vale Housing Estate, which lies in the Tame Valley, may be described as an island on its own. To the east runs the river Tame and on the west is the A38. The Chester Road became its southern border and the Birmingham to Derby Railway line lies to the north.

The area is steeped in history dating back to medieval times when the Cistercians owned it from Leicester Abbey. Before the war it was home to Castle Bromwich Aerodrome and spectacular Air Shows were held there. Mr Mortiboys, a resident of Castle Bromwich once told me that when he was a young boy he would sit on nearby Castle Hills and watch the planes carry out their acrobatics including, "Loop the loop."

This was the time before the motorway network and constant flow of traffic.

During the war the airfield was where the newly built planes, the Spitfires and Hurricanes were tested. The planes were built in what is now the Jaguar car factory. They were hauled across the road to the airfield where they were then tested. If there were no problems the planes were transported to various military airfields through out England. Maurice Horton and Ted Essex inform me that the Ferry pilots used in the transporting were mainly women and Maurice told me that one of them was the famous American pilot, Amy Johnson!

It is quite daunting to think that these planes were not armed at the time and the Ferry pilots were very vulnerable indeed. The airfield was technically still a civilian and not a military airfield. There is a story, which maybe apocryphal that goes like this.

One foggy night the engines of a big plane could be heard. The spluttering of the engines and its irregular rhythm more than suggested that the plane was in distress. The landing lights of the runway were turned on to assist the landing of the plane. A bulky bomber soon emerged from the fog and landed rather bumpily on the runway. However, to every one's amazement, there on the runway was a German bomber, a Heinkel! Apparently, so the story goes no one was quite sure what to do. Someone in the air control tower telephoned for the Home Guard. However, before the Home Guard could arrive on the scene, the plane's engines throbbed back into life and the plane sped down the runway, took off and disappeared into the foggy night.

No one is quite sure how true the story is but the residents of Castle Vale were more than clear in telling their memories.

June Freeth.

I lived in Sheldon where Birmingham airport is now. I remember the night Coventry was bombed. * I watched it from my bedroom window. I was only a child at the time. The sky was so light you could read a book by it. The raid lasted thirteen hours, non-stop, and it went through the night and into the next day. I just watched the flames; I could see the flames from Sheldon as Coventry was going down.

A few days later, my Dad who was a lorry driver took my Mother and me to Coventry. All I could remember was seeing Lady Godiva's statue still standing and all the shops and houses around it flattened.

Some of the shops had escaped and the shopkeepers were sweeping up the glass and boarding the windows up. If you went inside they were all dark, as there wasn't any electricity. They opened for business and sold what they got.

I remember the night when my sister was born. There was a heavy raid that night as the planes were looking for the airport. I remember going down into the shelter with my baby sister; she was only about seven hours old. My Mom, in her Black Country accent said, "Don't yow drop that babby!"

George Morris.

During the war years I was around many places including RAF Fighter Command. I was in London for about two years and I remember the fire of London very well indeed.

I was staying in Fore Street in the East End. After one of the fires and there were many at the time, there was a fire station still standing and the firemen had written on it, **THE ROCK OF GIBRALTAR**. Sandbags were holding it up.

I was later stationed at Wittering, in Rutland, near Peterborough, and I remember when they used to shoot German aircraft down and later rebuild them and fly them around the base. They wanted to find out more about them.

*It was the night of 14th November 1940 that the blitz began on Coventry. To this day many people still say, "I remember the night when Coventry got hit."

Also while I was stationed at Wittering, I was riding down the Great North Road and I saw a Blenheim plane only a few hundred yards away, when it suddenly stopped in mid air. I was only a few hundred yards from it. The plane was obviously about a mile from the camp and he was trying to turn around and as he did, it stopped in mid air. It then nose dived straight into the deck. There was a big explosion as the shells went off and the bullets too. It was impossible to get out. The fire tenders were soon on the scene, as were the, "Blood Wagons"** as they used to call them.

I couldn't get too near to it but I did see it afterwards. I could see the pilot and the navigator sitting down in the cockpit burnt to death. They were just sitting there as if they were still flying but they had been burnt to death, they were finished.

Coventry was hit again severely in April 1941. The blitz ended in May 1941 when most of the Luftwaffe transferred operations to the Eastern Front.

Bill Humphries.

I was enlisted in the army in 1943; I joined the PBI, "Poor Bloody Infantry." I was trained as a Bren gunner, until I went abroad and I went on a mines and explosive course. I was driving an ambulance jeep with two stretchers over head and one on the side. We used to pick the wounded up and went into the front line, pick them up, put them on the stretchers and bring them back to the Regimental Aid Post.

I was shot at by our own planes one day when I was in an ambulance convoy and I got caught in a gun barrage with our own guns.

After we had been in France three weeks I had three casualties on the ambulance and we were driving down a sunken road. I could hear tanks coming towards me. I didn't know whose tanks they were. With the dust from the tanks and the dark night I couldn't see a thing. I didn't know what to do. I turned on my headlights and then flashed my headlights and the tank stopped about 12 inches from me. What I said to the officer can not be repeated.

Nickname for Ambulances.

I took the wounded back and I was going down a road with a hedge on either side. As I wasn't too sure where I was going I drove very slowly. Then suddenly, a German soldier jumped from behind the hedge shouting, "Kamarad, kamarad."

I shouted back, "Kommen sie hier." I took him on the jeep and he was made a Prisoner of War.

When in Belgium coming along a sunken road with some wounded. I was being shelled and on top of the banks the shells were breaking. As I was low down I carried on driving. I suddenly felt something on my shoulder. I turned around to see that it was blood. One of the wounded above me had been hit and was bleeding on me. I managed to get him back safely.

I remember driving through Brenen, Germany, and seeing the church standing in the centre but everything around it was flattened. Also I was going through German lines when a German nurse approached me holding a white flag. She wanted to get some old people out on the German side. So they sent me in the jeep. She got on the jeep and as we drove she held the flag up. We went through our own lines and then we got to the German lines. I didn't see any German troops and as we crossed into the German lines all the firing stopped. I never heard a sound. However, there wasn't anyone to be found so we went back to our lines. As soon as we got back there the guns opened up again.

I was blown up six days before VE Day, 2nd May 1945, The only thing that saved me was the skid chains in the jeep under the controls that took the full blast of the mine.
I had every bone in my ankle and foot broken.

Bill was part of the final onslaught, the "Race to the Rhine" in order to meet the Russians who were advancing from the East. March 1945 saw Operation Plunder take place where Airborne Divisions landed east of the Rhine. Soon after Field Marshall Montgomery successfully crossed the Rhine at Wesel. The end of the war was in sight.

Cecile Dyer.

My brother Albert had registered to join up. He wanted to be a pilot. He didn't have the necessary educational qualifications so he went to join the Marines. The Marine Sergeant said to him said, "Look son, if you were a lad of mine I wouldn't advise you to join the Marines. We're after the rough tough type." Albert was only a kid and he looked like a kid. "Blow you then." He said, "I'll join the Monkey Outfit." The monkey outfit was the Navy so he went off and joined the Royal Navy.

He trained at HMS Arthur at the old Skegness Holiday camp. They couldn't find a hat small enough for him. When he did get a hat he had to pack it full of newspaper before it would fit. He also had brittle teeth so they took his top teeth out.

He then went on an electrical training course. Out of a hundred who took the course only three passed and Albert was one of them. He was now a Leading Wireman. He was then sent to Scotland where he was in charge of landing barges for commandos. There were three naval personnel who looked after all the barges and commandos.

He later went to Liverpool and was posted on a ship called the SS Strathnava, an Indian Ocean ship that had been turned into a troop carrier. When he got on board he noticed that the ship was full of Canadians. He used to write home, "Dear Mom, I can't tell you where I am but I am with…." The rest would be then cut out. There wasn't a sentence that wasn't partly cut out.

Albert travelled down the West Coast of Africa back up the East Coast, through the Suez Canal and on to Cairo. They took the excess baggage off the ship and filled it full of troops. The ship then sailed for the Mediterranean and they were involved in the Sicily landings. They made the first landing in the barge and then the ship broke down. He lost one of his shoes during the landing. As he didn't have any replacements he threw the other one after it!

The ship limped back to Liverpool. They were anxious sailing through the Med, as it was full of U-boats. It took three days and when he got back he was relieved but realised that he didn't have any shoes on!

He sent a telegram to his Mom that he was home and then he asked the dockers if they had any old shoes he could have. They found him a pair but they were size eleven and had a hole in them. To make matters worse, Albert's shoe size was seven! He had to stuff them full of newspaper and put cardboard where the toes were. When he walked up the path of the house, Mom shouted, "Al's here. Al's here." We hadn't seen him for about eight months. That evening the telegram came to say that he was coming home.

During D-Day he was going backwards and forwards across the channel laying smoke screens. He also told me that he used to take secret agents to France and drop them off on the coast. He was always reticent about telling me.

Gladys Adams.

I was 18 when I got married. I married a lad called Frank Adams. Just before I got married we were bombed and all the ceilings came down. My entire wedding outfit was in the house. The Air Raid Wardens said that I couldn't go back in to get it. However, my brother did go and get my wedding outfit and take it to my mother-in-law to be.

We got married in the big church in Handsworth and had the wedding reception at my mother-in-law's. Everything was going lovely but then we heard the sirens and were told to go down the shelters, but we didn't bother and carried on with the reception!

Anyway, after the raid we were getting ready to go to our new home in Warley. I was looking forward to it when suddenly the sirens went off again. We had to spend our wedding night at his Mom's'.

I had bought myself a satin green nightdress, I thought it was lovely. As I was staying at his Mom's the nightie was out of the question so I wore one of his Mom's instead. It had all big frills. I wouldn't get into bed. I made Frank get out first before I got in. We were very shy in those days! There were only two bedrooms. We were in a single bed in the corner and on the other side of the room were some of the wedding guests in a double bed! We had a marvellous time!

The next day we went back to Warley.

Joan Day.

I was 16 and lived in Fulham, London, during the war and we would watch dogfights taking place in the sky above, between the Germans and the English. I used to stand in the street and watch them, I didn't think of the danger. It was fascinating watching two planes fighting each other above the streets of Fulham. I didn't think at the time that there were two men trying to kill each other, I just thought it was fascinating, standing there watching them in the sky.

One day on my way to work I came across a cinema that had been bombed. They reckoned that there were three hundred people in there and all of them were killed.

I joined the WRAF. We trained at Wilmslow in Cheshire. I went to Heywood near Manchester. There were Jamaican airmen there and as I was a cook I used to serve them their meals. They used to eat at different times. The authorities said it was because of different diets, but I wonder. Some of the white airmen objected to a Jamaican serving in the kitchens so he was moved. It was silly considering we were supposed all to be on the same side.

I met one of the Jamaican airmen. He was a solicitor and when he returned to the West Indies he wrote me a letter. He sent it to my parents' home. My uncle told me that it had arrived from Jamaica but I never got to read it. It went all around the camps before it got to my home address and by that time I was just about to get married.

I was then stationed in Moreton - in - Marsh in Gloucestershire. When the bombers used to come back from the raids all they wanted was egg and bacon. So we used to have to open the cookhouse up in the middle of the night just so they could have egg and bacon. They would all eat in the Airmen's Mess, officers and all.

There was the Airmen's Mess, the Sergeants' Mess and the Officers' Mess. If you went into an Officers' Mess it was like going into a posh hotel. They had everything, while the Airmen's Mess had bread and jam! I worked in the Airmen's Mess. After a raid they would notice those that hadn't made it back. They would look at one another and hope that they would be back later or had landed in the country somewhere. But quite a lot didn't make it, mainly the air gunners, as they had so little protection. All the time I was there I never saw an aeroplane.

Bryan Newman.

I was born in 1933, so when the war started I was six years old.

My first memory of the war is that I was with my Mum in Lozells Road, Aston, watching a very long parade of soldiers marching. It was just like a river of khaki moving the whole length of the road, from Villa Cross right down to Six Ways. It probably went a lot further but that is what I could see.

I remember the people thousands of them, cheering these men in khaki uniforms as they marched. I didn't know what all this was about, it was just fun and excitement to me.

We grew up so fast in those days, because of the war, and it wasn't long before I did know what it was all about. Those men that I had seen marching were going to fight for our country. None of them knew whether they would be alive in a couple of months' time or not. They were brave men, but I don't think any of them considered themselves brave. To them it was war and they were going to fight for England.

For some time after that I can remember my Dad and my uncles coming home and going away very frequently and they too were all dressed in khaki uniform. Except my Uncle Ted who was dressed in a blue uniform. He was in the navy.

Little did I know that they were doing very dangerous jobs. None of them ever knew from one day to the next when their lives would come to an end. Come to think of it all of us, all the civilians, wives, sweethearts, children, the people left at home, whilst their loved ones went to fight, were also in danger from the bombing. No one really knew whether they would see daylight the next day.

I can remember those air raids, with all the noise and people shouting to get down the shelters. There were all kinds of shelters. The Anderson shelter, which was usually in the garden, dug right down into the earth and then was covered with soil. There would be steps down to the entrance and inside it was just like a bedroom with bunks to sleep on. Whenever you went to the shelters you always had to take your bedding with you.

Not everyone had a shelter, so people used to share with neighbours. Other people would bed down under the stairs in the house, which was said to be as safe as a shelter, which proved to be true. My Mum used to put my sisters and me under the stairs as soon as the sirens went and then she would go and do her duties as an Air Raid Warden. That was until we had a table shelter. This was an indoor shelter, all steel with wire mesh sides, just like a cage really. It was used as a table during the day and a shelter at night. We always thought it was great fun sleeping under the table, although we were caged like animals. It was for our own safety.

I can remember one night when my mum took me out on to the doorstep to watch baskets of flares coming down from the sky. The German planes were dropping them.

I don't think I had much idea at the time what all this was about. I wasn't quite aware that people were trying to kill us, although I knew that people were being killed.

You would hear people talking and saying, "Did you know so and so caught it last night?"

I knew one thing though; all the people who went into the shelters or stayed with friends or relatives, everyone you met and talked to were always in high spirits. Those Germans didn't frighten our mums and aunts. In the shelters they kept everyone's spirits up by singing, joking and trying to ignore the bombing that was going on. Although they would often say, 'That was a close one.'

Everyone must have been worried about losing someone, but they covered this up and never showed fear.

I remember one of the communal shelters having a direct hit. This shelter housed probably a couple of dozen people. On this occasion about eight or nine people were killed, all neighbours of ours. Everyone was horrified at what had happened but no one gave up hope that one day we would win the war.

After every raid, which was now nightly, you always found out that someone you had known had died the night before. Even as a small boy, I was now learning what it was all about.

I remember our school was bombed. We all thought that it was great until we were told that we had to go to people's homes to take our lessons. I went to this house in Lozells Street with about six other kids. We didn't enjoy the best of teaching methods. We just used to get a book and read it, or get a piece of paper and a pencil and do some sums on it. If you did that everyone was happy. We all enjoyed ourselves though. At least as a family we were not split up, like a lot of other families.

A lot of children were evacuated to the country: it was said that it was safer than living in the city. My Mum took my sister and me to live at a public house in the town centre, 'The Sun' at the corner of Sun Street. Not a good idea really when you knew that all the other kids were moving out of the city to be safe.

But you didn't question your parents as you knew that mum would not put you in danger and anywhere that mum went we wanted to be with her. We didn't want to go to the country not knowing when we would return, if ever. Our other sister was older than us and was in the Red Cross, so we didn't see much of her at all.

When we lived at the Sun Public House, it wasn't for long, because that too was hit by a bomb. A bomb that went straight though the roof of the snooker room. I remember that one of the barmaids was killed that night whilst on her way home from work.

After that I lived with my grandmother in Lozells Street, right opposite the school I went to. My cousin Alf also lived with us, he was just two years older than me, but went to the same school.

Gran had a large family, ten children. So I had lots of aunts and uncles who were always visiting her house. In fact the home always seemed to be full of people. It was a large house with stables at the rear and a yard where Granddad kept all kinds of animals.

One day I was at school, just a few yards away from where I lived and the teacher told me that I was wanted in the corridor. So I went to have a look to see who wanted me. It was my uncle. He had told the teacher that he was my dad and that he had a 24-hour pass. I got the afternoon off school.

I lived with my Gran for a couple of years, so did Alf, so it was like having a brother. At school everyone thought that we were brothers as we were both named Newman.
Alf was a big lad, his nickname was Fatty, and for quite a time I thought that was his name. Not many kids tangled with Fatty so I never got any stick from anyone, as they thought he was my brother.

I remember when lorries drove around all the streets and collected any iron that they saw. If your garden gates were iron they took them. No one minded. This iron was collected for the war effort. If we were to win the war then all this iron was needed. It was quite a sight seeing men pull down gates, railings, fences anything that would help in the war effort.

I can also remember all the older men and women who were thought to be too old to fight in the front line. They became the Home Guard and Air Raid Wardens and they became a very important part of the Home Defence. They would do this after they had done a day's work in the ammunition factories. If the Germans had invaded, not one of these people would have surrendered. So terrific was the spirit of the British people. Worried stiff about loved ones fighting for our country and yet still giving all to defend it. Words can't really describe the togetherness of all the people.

I remember going to Sutton Park and that's where I saw some prisoners of war behind barbed wire working on the land. In fact they gave us some potatoes to take home. These people didn't seem like killers to me. In fact I don't think we ever thought they were, (as kids). We laughed at them because they were prisoners of war. I don't think we kids knew what that meant at the time.

I remember when Mum was serving behind the pub and the place was full of servicemen, as it always was. She heard from someone about the ship my Dad was on. He was going to North Africa and apparently a torpedo had hit the ship but we didn't know how true this was. Most of the information that came back with these men was usually true.

She didn't know whether he had survived or not. She must have been under a tremendous amount of stress. But she didn't show this to my sister and me. I understand that she didn't want us to know about it until she knew for certain what had happened. Thank goodness, it was a couple of weeks later that we heard that he had been hit but had survived and was plucked from the sea by another ship.

It then came out that a torpedo has also hit this ship, but again Dad survived by being able to swim for a few hours, a long distance to the shores of Tunisia. This is where he spent the rest of the war fighting with the First and the Eighth armies.

In the meantime I remember when we had a bomb land in our back garden and Mum put out the fire on her own.

The people who stayed at home to defend our land were never really recognised. They were the most dedicated of people, with no pay, and without them I don't know what would have happened. They certainly kept the Home Fires Burning.

It makes me so angry when footballers and celebrities are called 'Heroes'. Have all these brave people been forgotten? They were all heroes.

Gwen Cooper.

In 1939 I was sixteen year of age and working as a sewing machinist in Ladywood. I remember going to work one morning after a heavy raid and was told a landmine had been dropped in the Cregro Street area.

In our lunch hour one or two of the girls and myself decided to go and have a look. That was when we realised what damage these bombs could do. The whole of a wide area ahead was completely flat, with hardly a brick standing.

St Thomas School and church was also bombed and I often wondered how many of the girls I went to school with survived, because most of them lived around that area.

The cellar of our house had been reinforced so that is where we stayed during the air raids. My father used to go fire watching. Another night after a heavy raid my father came and told us the Market Hall and the Bull Ring had had a direct hit. I went out into the street and it was just as if the whole city centre was on fire.

We lived just off Broad Street by Five Ways, so we weren't too far away. I remember the Air Raid Warden shouting at me to go down the shelter as the air raid was still on, but at that age I didn't realise the danger from shrapnel.

When I was about eighteen years old the government decided I should be helping the war effort. I was given the choice of the forces or working in a factory. I chose a factory and was found a job in a small factory near where I lived, making elevators* for aircraft. After about three months I was sent for by the personnel officer, who offered me a job as progress chaser. This meant going around to all the different departments and making sure they weren't waiting for parts.

The young man who had been doing the job was called up for the forces. I loved this job and thought this would be where I would stay, but once again the Labour Exchange told me I could be doing more. So I was ordered to do A.R.P or fire service duty once a week. So I joined the fire service and was stationed at Albion Street, Aston, as a telephonist.

* Tail end of aeroplanes.

I went on duty straight from work at seven o'clock and stayed all night, (praying there wouldn't be any air raids). I had to be back at work at 7.30 the next morning.

I must have been one of the unlucky ones because once again I was sent for and was told a younger person could do my job and I would have to go back into the factory, which is where I stayed.

In 1944 I met a soldier, Arthur Cooper, who had just returned from the Middle East. We married in March 1945. We had one ten-day embarkation leave together and then he went to Palestine, where he stayed for 12 months. He came home to be demobbed.

I was still working in the factory and wanted to leave and go back to my sewing job but before I could I had to go to a tribunal and tell them the reasons. It was all a load of red tape, but I did get their permission.

I have never met anyone who was called up so many times for war work as me. It was now 1947 and my husband was home, I had no problem leaving the fire service and I finally went back to my pre-war job and met again some of the girls (now women) I had worked with before the war.

James Farrell.

I was seven years old and I was preparing to make my first Holy Communion one morning in 1942 when a German plane dropped bombs over the North Strand in Dublin. The story was that the bombs were meant for Belfast but they dropped them too soon. Belfast was seen as the backdoor of England and the Germans wanted to destroy the docks.

 I heard the fire brigade and ambulance so I ran down the road to see what all the commotion was about. I saw people running all over the place. I followed them. The bombing was a good few streets away. Then I saw all the houses and shops flattened. They were pulling people out, the dead and injured. I stood watching my mother was looking for me all over. When she found me, we were all crying and wanting to go home.

I went to church, which is on Garnier Street in the centre of Dublin. A few hours later I made my first Holy Communion. They said that 37 people had died and a lot of people were injured.

The Germans sent a letter of apology to the people of Dublin; it was in all the papers.

Teresa Farrell (Nee Nolan.)

I was just a small child in Dublin when the war was on. It wasn't as bad as England with the bombings, but there were rations and shortages of fruit. I didn't know what a banana tasted like until after the war and I got my first one.

Nearly all our dads were in England in the war. My dad, Thomas Nolan, went before the war to work in the mines. My family lived in one room and he used to send money home. When the war broke out he went into a munitions factory in Peterborough. He was also an ARP Warden and at night he went around making sure everyone's windows were blacked out.

Back in Dublin we were all worried. We hated to see the telegram boy coming in case it was bad news. I would keep asking mum when dad was coming home, because I was to make my first Holy Communion. But he didn't come home until after the war was over.

He came home on a stretcher off the boat in Dublin. He wasn't injured but he had T.B and he was very ill. He went straight into hospital. When my mother came home from the hospital with his case we opened it up. All you could see was chocolate bars on top of his clothes. He had saved his rations up for us.

He was two years in hospital, but he told us all about the war. Years after we all came to Birmingham.

He had good memories of people he met in the war. When I got married the first house I lived in was in Aston, Six Ways. In 1959 it still had an air raid shelter in the back yard.

Len Beaman.

The war started off in France in the Maginot line and the Siegfried line and as you all know our forces were pushed right back to the beaches and we all remember Dunkirk.

We then had to defend ourselves and feed ourselves. We had our fighting forces but we had lost such a lot of trained men and women that the L.D.V or Homeguard was formed and also the ARP.

Children were evacuated by being sent into the country to be looked after by strangers and quite a few children were drowned at sea going to America.

Orders were given that all men and women were to be called up either for the forces or the land army. Everyone was told to dig for victory, to grow your own food.

A lot of men called Bevin boys were sent down the coalmines, as coal in those days was our main source of energy. Mr Churchill asked for the tools to finish the job, so nearly all women had to go into the factories to get the tools. We had men and women come from Ireland, from up Scotland and Wales to work in the Midlands. A lot of them worked on transport to keep everything moving.

Not long before the bombing started it was down into the shelters, unless you were working or on duty. People were working by day and on duty by night, or working by night and on duty by day.

While this was going on men and women in the forces were training for either the army or the airforce and all this time we had our gallant navy and merchant navy carrying supplies to and fro across the dangerous oceans.

D-Day came and all our front line men and women were off to do battle, and sadly many of them never returned.

We must not forget all our men and women who were prisoners of war and those who were fighting in other parts of the war.

We were glad we had allies from other countries here on our side, then finding victory was ours, but we must never forget our dead forces and civilians.

I think we are still as proud of our country today as we were then and we are glad that we still have lots of our foreign friends with us.

Frank Flanner resident of Whitehouse Common, Sutton Coldfield.

I was in the police messenger service during the war. They decided to take the senior boy scouts and give them a course in Air Raid, gas precautions and First Aid. We had to do a test and then we were issued with a certificate. CCH Moriarty, The Chief Constable of Birmingham, signed it 26th May 1939.

You had to have a bike and go to the nearest police station. Mine was Duke Street in the city centre. We would wait there for any messages to come in. They were then to be carried to various police stations in the vicinity in the event of communication breakdown due to bomb damage. I was involved in taking messages to Victoria Road, Aston. It was a bit horrendous at times with bombs falling around and you did not know if you would cycle into a hole or not.

I did have an experience when I was working in the city post office. I was on an early shift and I was walking down from my house into the street when a lady popped her head over a garden wall. She said, "Frank, would you mind coming to have a look at a hole in the roof that goes down into my bedroom and down into the kitchen, below. I think an incendiary bomb has gone down there, from the raid last night"

I went to have a look; sure enough there was a hole, but a not very big one. I said I would report it to the police or the ARP. I reported it and the authorities came down and it turned out to be a 500 pound unexploded bomb. If it had gone off I wouldn't be here talking to you today.

The bomb disposal squad came down and they cleared all the streets and then went into the house and steamed the mechanism out of the bomb. They put some planks on the front of the house and onto the street. We were looking from a lamp post about a hundred yards down the street. If it had gone off we would have been killed! Half the street was there. They put ropes around the bomb and they pulled it through the front window. The rope went all the way down the street and around a lamppost where we were standing. They were pulling on it and gradually the bomb came out and was made useless.

That was one of my main experiences. The other was the bombing of Blews Street Park. They bombed the shelter and a policeman and quite a few people in the shelter were killed. But the blast blew my father and me (we were just round the corner) about twenty yards down the road.

We lived in a state of tension all the while, never knowing whether we were going to survive the next three or four hours. At home all the windows were blown out so many times that we had to put gauze on the windows, like most people did because you couldn't keep replacing the glass.

One evening, my father and I were outside watching to see what was happening, when an incendiary bomb came down and hit the little shop on the corner of our entry and bounced off. We didn't know what was going to happen, because at that time they were charging the incendiary Bombs with explosives. They exploded if you went near them. We ran to the factory across the road, picked up a couple of sandbags and threw them over the bomb, to make sure we wouldn't get hurt. Luckily it never went off.

There were lots of fires going on and one quite amusing thing was that the fireman came and they put their hosepipes up. There was a brook which runs down Aston Brook Street and they put the end in to draw the water out and all that happened was a little dribble came out of the hose at the other end. So they had to get the water from the engine itself and other places.

The police didn't give me my uniform until the year I joined the forces in 1941. Until then all I had was a police helmet, which was a blue one and it used to come down over my ears when I put it on, as I was only five-foot nothing. And every time I saw a light, I used to knock the door and say 'Put that light out' and they'd say 'Get away you little urchin'. I was about eighteen then.

I saw more action in Birmingham during the war than I did in the whole of my five years in the forces.

I went from being a Police Messenger to the RAF. I joined up because I wanted to be a wireless operator. I had to go down to Cardington near London for flying duty selection. But unfortunately I failed the medical for the flying, because of chest trouble. So I pleaded with them to be a wireless operator on the ground.

" What makes you want to be a wireless operator" ' they said.
So I said that my father in the First World War was a sergeant wireless operator in the Warwickshire Regiment.

So they said to me "So he was in the signals?"

I said 'Yes'.

So the RAF sergeant took me to the officer in charge and said, "This man wants to be a wireless operator because his father was."

"Ok we'll take you then," came the reply.

Anyway I had a six months wait, then I went to Blackpool for the first part of my wireless course and 'square bashing' and all that sort of thing. The second part of the course was down in Compton Bassett, Wiltshire. After I passed out I went to a Bomber Station RAF Thurleigh, near Bedford. We didn't know at the time that it was going to be taken over by the American Airforce for Flying Fortresses. So they shipped everybody out. I was posted to India.

I sailed from Liverpool in the Duchess of Bedford on 15th April 1942. By that time we had been singled out into groups of fifty. But we didn't know what we were going to do.

There were three of us in our group who were wireless operators. But there were lots of others wearing 'sparks' in our group but we couldn't understand why they were there. We soon found out. They were Canadians. It wasn't until we got near to Bombay that we were told that they were Radar Mechanics and Operators because Radar was extremely secret at that time. We had a Canadian Sergeant in charge of us. We went via West Africa and Durban, South Africa. We couldn't go through the Mediterranean because of the war there.

During the journey a Cruiser came alongside, wanting to speak to the Captain. They told him to turn round and put in to Mombassa, East Africa, Kenya. When we got there the whole of the Eastern fleet was there. It was a marvellous sight. I was ill with a fever at that time, and had to go into the sickbay. But they opened the side of the ship and I could see all the fleet and everything. Subsequently we learned that the change of plan was that we might have been wanted for the war in the Middle East.

From there we went to India, Bombay, where we went to another camp and we were shunted off to Madras to another little holding unit. The Radar people, the Canadians, went a further hundred miles to French India, in Southeast India, Pondicherry, to set up the station.

Whilst in Madras I read about the terrible devastation that Birmingham suffered due to the bombing. I remember reading the 'Madras Indian Express' on July 29th 1942. This is what the headlines said,

"FULL MOON RAIDERS OVER BRITAIN. WAVES OF PLANES ATTACK BIRMINGHAM. FAIRLY NUMEROUS CASUALTIES.

The report went on to say,

"The Germans say that Birmingham had a heavy air raid and that some of the heaviest bombs were dropped on the city.
According to German accounts the Germans sent over 200 bombers."

I was very worried about my family and friends back home.

I was left in Madras with three other wireless operators, until the station was ready to become operational. Whilst I was operating on the radio in Madras, somebody came on the frequency in Morse Code and said 'Please send us some bloody wireless operators to Pondicherry, so we can become operational'. So we had to go to Pondicherry, a hundred miles away. That was 268 AMES, (Air Ministry Experimental Station).

We had some fun down there. I was sitting on the radio set one night, and a message came through in code. It was, " 'X Rush' Jap invasion imminent. Get ready to blow up your aerials and equipment, and retreat to a place that has been specially designed for you."

We didn't know where that actually was. So we panicked as we only had 15 rifles for 50 of us. We passed on the message to the C.O. and he said, " Oh I didn't know anything about this, I will go and see the British Consul in Pondicherry." So off he went to see him. At the same time we had an aircraft coming across, which wasn't showing whether it was friendly or not. It didn't show the IFF (Information Friend or Foe) signal, which would show up on the monitor screen of the Radar. As it wasn't sending one out, we panicked. But it turned out it was all right.

The C.O. came back down the country lane in his jeep, waving a piece of paper in his hand like Neville Chamberlain. "It's all right, it's all right!" he shouted. It turned out it was an army exercise. The first two groups of the message were 'X Rush', which in army code means it's an exercise and at that time there was no liasing between signals, Army, Airforce and Navy.

When I was away in India, letters used to take three months to reach us, to begin with. Then the air-graph came out. People back home were able to go into the post office and get a form, fill it in, and then they would photograph it and send it on a 35mil negative and send it out to various forces. They would reproduce it full size and it took 4 days, so the post went from three months to 4 days from England to India. Fabulous!

The Japanese were threatening to invade India and they had already had a go at Sri Lanka. We were there to protect India from the Japanese.

The Radar station in Pondicherry closed down after about two years, and I was moved up to Bangalore, which was headquarters of the 225 group. I was operating from there, very high-powered transmitters in touch with the UK, Australia and all round.

I was sitting on the set one night and I couldn't hear a blooming thing and thought, "That's strange!" And so the next morning the signal came up saying, "What have you been doing all night? Have you been asleep?" Nobody had told me that I should have changed the frequency to what was called the 'Night frequency'. I wasn't there very long after that!

They posted me again. In the words of the signals officer, "Do you want a nice cushy job?" he said, "Right by the sea side, it's a convalescent home really." And I was posted there with one or two others. It was a place called Korangi Creek near Karachi, and a flying boat base.

Whilst there I managed to get Sand fly fever; it's like malaria and I nearly died. The only thing that saved my life was the first arrival of penicillin in India.

Our Signals Officer shot himself. He was going to marry a nurse, and he came in one day into the office and asked how many messages we had had. He then went to his office and shot himself. The bullet went straight through his head and nearly hit one of our blokes on duty and hit the post office wall outside. Allegedly the reason was that he was due to marry this girl, and it was said he had been fiddling the mess funds and he was going to get married on the funds, but he couldn't take it, so he shot himself.

I was there until I was re-patriated in 1945. I really enjoyed it there. They recommended me for sergeant only a month before I came back home but I didn't want to move my digs from the airman's quarters to the sergeants' Mess and start all over again. I am a wireless operator through and through and still do my Morse code in 'civvy street', as a licensed radio amateur, call sign 'G 3 AVE'. I am a member of the Radio Society of Great Britain and the R.A.F. Amateur Radio Society.

Anyway I came back to the UK at Christmas 1945 on the, 'Queen of Bermuda.' There were a lot of ex-prisoners of war from Japan on board. One of the organists on the Odeon circuit, a bloke called Con Doherty used to play the piano on board. It was lovely listening to him, going through the sea at night time. You could look over the side and see all the different fish, glowing, very nice it was. The war was over so it was great to see everything 'lit up'.

So that was that, and I came back to the UK and they posted me to Honiley near Coventry. They had no jobs for wireless operators, as it was all done by Tele-printers by then and I hadn't really handled a Tele-printer much. So I told the signal officer there that I used to operate Tele-printers and he said 'Just the man, you can take charge of the midnight shift' I was a corporal then.

You forget the bad moments, because of your friends. I enjoyed my life in the forces.
Being a wireless operator was what I really wanted to do and that's what I did!

Corporal Frank Flanner, RAF Radio Operator in India

Corporal Frank Flanner, (front row, third on right) and fellow wireless operators from 212 Squadron under mosquito nets at Korangi Creek, Karachi 1943. Front row, first left sits Ken Pritchard who was from Yardley, Birmingham.

"We do like to be by the seaside!"
Pondicherry, South East India, 1942.
Frank Flanner is second from left back row.

Violet Horsely resident of Walmley Sutton Coldfield.

I was fifteen years old when the war started and I was working because we left school at fourteen. When I was about sixteen and a half I worked for the Co-op Milk, driving a horse and cart.

Then I thought that I ought to do something more than this, so I applied to go into the ATS. They wouldn't release me at first as I was already doing a man's job. Anyway after two or three tries they said all right and I joined the ATS which was the Auxiliary Territorial Service, which later became the WRAC.

I did my training at Northampton. We all wanted to do driving of course, but there weren't enough vacancies so we were told we were going into 'Ack Ack' or signals. So I went into Ack Ack. I went to Park Hall Camp where they did all the training and then I did quite a few months at Anglesey, St Johns Point where we did our training for firing the guns. (We didn't actually fire the guns by the way, the men did). We did our training there and they had what they call a sleeve at the back of the plane, and the sleeve had to be fired at, not the plane. And from there we went to Ireland for twelve months. Of course, there wasn't anything doing there, no raids, anything like that. But nevertheless it was hard work. Then from there we came to Firth, by Gosport and that was when a lot of the 'Doodle Bugs' were being dropped. That would be 1944 by then.

We were then sent to Brighton. We stayed in Civilian Billets at Brighton and our camp was on a golf course. The other girls in my unit were lovely. There were about twenty girls, Riggy was my closest friend, and she lived in Kendal. Then there was Betty Emberson, and Dimps Goodyear who lived in Ilfracombe. Her real name was Doris Goodyear, but we called her Dimps.

We had a lot of nasty mishaps on the south coast. Needless to say some of them were very sad. But we were just doing our job. It was very frightening at times, because these guns were heavy Ack Ack guns, which made a terrific noise.

I was on the height finder; we had a predictor, a height finder and a spotter that were actually on the command posts. The GL and radiolocation was underneath the command posts.

So if we saw the planes, the spotter would say "Plane", and we'd go for it. One would take the bearing whilst another would take the height, and then I would analyse the information and say 'Bearing so and so, height so and so ' but before that happened I would look through the sight, which is a long apparatus on stilts. I would look through this little sight and then I would see the plane and say 'Right'. When the girls got the plane in their vision, I would shout 'Height finder on target' and then I would say 'Height so and so bearing so and so' and I would analyse the two. And then hopefully we would get the accuracy of the height and the bearings. When the height matched the predictor the commanding officer would shout, "Fire" and the guns were automatically fired.

The guns were a matter of yards from us and they were in concrete bunkers. We were on the command post. But the sounds of the guns were very loud. They were big, full-size guns. In the night, during a raid, we could be called out of our billets. When we returned because of the damage from the bombs, all our things would have come off the shelves. We would straighten everything up, get into bed but probably be out again in the next half-hour.

We also had to take turns on the searchlight. None of us liked it on the searchlight, but we had to take our turn. Well, I always felt that the plane was going to come down the light, I thought it's going to come down the beam and bombard me with bullets! Then we had to do aircraft recognition, so we knew which plane we were shooting at. Now the Stuka Dive Bombers were very frightening. Hopefully we never shot at our people, which I don't think we did.

I remember one night when we shot a German plane down. It was a Dornier. We watched it come down. It was quite a way from us. It didn't damage our post, but we were near enough to see what had happened. We wanted to shout and cheer because we had shot this plane down. But we couldn't, as we had to wait until the All Clear sounded and then we cheered.

If people said they weren't frightened then I think they would be telling lies. Because I know I was frightened as I was thinking of them bombing my family. So you think, well if I don't get them, they are going to get us. But I think if people were truthful there was always fear about. I mean a lot of our girls got killed, not necessarily on the site where I was. There was one raid, and I'm not sure where it was, but I believe there was quite a few killed, at least eleven. And I remember one night we were running down to the command post and Vera Littler, who came from Loughborough, fell over and we couldn't stop to pick her up. We had to leave her there, hoping she'd be all right. She just tripped I think, was still half-asleep or hadn't done the laces up on her boots or something like that. We had to leave her, but fortunately she was all right and she soon came hobbling down towards the command post.

At night, for our entertainment, we used to have music in the NAAFI and have a dance until the sirens went. We women got on with the men. The Billets of course were separate, naturally. No hanky panky in those days! At least I didn't get up to any, I don't know if any one else did. We were on parade together and we did jobs together. We would go in the NAFI at lunchtime, and I had two or three good dancing partners. And they would say, "Come on Gibby, let's have a jive". It was wonderful. But they respected us, they never abused us, they never treated us badly, they never looked down on us. And there were a lot of men, a lot of them. Half ours were old enough to be my father because they were conscripted.

And the discipline! Actually we didn't mind the discipline, we knew what was expected of us and we abided by it. If you didn't you'd be in the 'What's it'.

I had a little friend who came from Billesley and her name was Emily Cheek, Emily Bertha Cheek, so we called her 'Cheeky B' (her initials you see). Now she stretched some of the officers to the limit and she used to get away with it she really did. I remember one day we were in Ireland and we had this big Brigadier coming. And all the paving stones round this pathway had to be painted white. And of course this went against the grain with Cheeky.

Someone came up behind and she didn't turn round. She went on and she said 'Oh go and get in your dog's kennel!' She turned around and there was the Brigadier, I think he was so dumb struck he didn't know what to do! And that's how she was. And they'd say 'Cheek, put that cigarette out', and she would turn round, but still carry on with it in her hand. Where I would have said 'Yes indeed'.

Bertha had ginger hair and she was just lovely. I wouldn't have said 'boo' to an officer or to a sergeant even. Although I was a very good friend with my sergeant, I always spoke to her as Sergeant until we came out of the army.

You could go days without having a day off duty. When it was heavy with D-day, and there was a lot of bombing and that, they would stop our leave, stop our days off.

We used to go to Brighton to what we called the 'Dome', which is the Pavilion. We used to go dancing there. And because it was more or less towards the end of the war, they allowed us to go in our civvies. I remember I had a pretty flowered dress and I felt like the Queen of Sheba, dancing around. It was wonderful, it really was wonderful. Something we hadn't experienced since we were teenagers.

I was twenty-one in 1945 and at that time a lot of the girls were younger than me.

I remember one girl, Mavis, she came from North Wales. And they found out after she had been in about twelve months that she was under age. I will always remember we cried because we didn't want her to go. But even then she was only about sixteen and she had been in quite a few months then.

All the nights were very bad and, as I say, it was frightening, but you didn't think about that, you just carried on. But the good things made up for the bad things. When we were spud - bashing and all that sort of thing we'd talk about what happened the night before and things like that. Because although you were on ack ack, you still had to do your duties, as silly as that seemed sometimes.

We slept in a wooden hut. We'd go to bed as normal and then wait for the sirens to go. We were far enough away from the command post. We were right on the front on the beaches and before D-day we were actually sleeping under canvas right by the command post, so we could be at action stations quicker than if we were up in the huts.

Towards the end of the war I might only see one or two planes in my area, but the worse things were the 'Doodle Bugs'* because when you heard the engines cut out you knew they were going to drop. I remember the first time we heard this one and it exploded not very far from us, but not near enough to hurt us. It was not far from Collingwood, which is a Naval Base at Farnham.

*Rockets called the V1, which proved to be very destructive.

The bombs stopped in 1945, just before May. May was VE Day and August was VJ Day. It is hard for people to visualise it and when I looked at the youngsters today I think 'I wish they would do more with their lives,' because we had to grow up very quickly. I think my wages were eleven shillings. I made a little allowance for my mother, because she was a widow.

I have kept in touch with quite a lot of my friends and sadly I have lost a few, but we have kept in touch all these years because the bond is there. When we go up to the reunions in York every year, the last week in July, well, it just tear jerks you, because it is such a wonderful feeling.

I still write to seven of them, if only Christmas cards now, but never the less. And a few years ago some of us met up in Chester. I booked a hotel and we had a few days in Chester. That was lovely, reminiscing. You can reminisce for years and years. I would hope that my grandchildren (well nobody) should ever experience a war. It's dreadful, completely dreadful.

Oh I missed my mum. I missed my sister. Because one of my sisters got very badly burned while I was in the army. And they got me some leave to see her. Her nightie caught fire. She got too near the fire didn't she. She was critically ill for a long time and she took her scars to the grave with her a few years ago. You know things like that. If someone phoned and said, "So and so is ill," you couldn't just say "Well I'll go and visit her." And my mother was also very ill, so they gave me a few months' leave. My officer, Miss Burgess, she gave me my train fare to get home. Things like that stick in your mind.

Violet Horsley during her ATS days.

My mother lived in Nechells so she was in Dudley Road Hospital. I got off at the station at Snow Hill with my kit bag and walked to Dudley Road Hospital. Which you wouldn't do now at two or three o'clock in the morning, would you?

I met my husband in the Nechells area, because I was in the ARP then and he was a home guard. He went into the Navy and I went in the Army.

He used to come home on leave, every leave he could get. Because being in the Navy he was abroad all the time. We made the best of a bad job. Where ever I was, if he got leave he would be there. In fact I think the officers got fed up with seeing him. I was so emotional, I mean you said, "Cheerio," and we didn't know if we would see each other again. It was the same with our families, we didn't know.

My happiest memory was VE day and after that VJ day. After the VE day Ack, Ack was disbanded and they didn't need us anymore. We were all split up. I went to Elstree Studios and I worked with the Ordnance Unit and we were in Civil Billets.

Violet and friends from ATS.

Mere Green Over Fifties Group, Sutton Coldfield.

Mere Green lies to the north of Sutton Town centre on the Lichfield Road. Sutton was home to a variety of military personnel during the Second World War including American GI's who worked at the American Postal Sorting Office. In Lichfield, a Battalion of African-American GI's was stationed and they occasionally visited Sutton.

Near Mere Green lies the very attractive and large Sutton Park. This was "Home" to a variety of German and Italian Prisoners of War. There was also a searchlight battery and the tragedy that surrounds it is told in another chapter.

The Mere Green Over Fifties group meets in the old Victorian village school, which is now a community centre. As with the ladies at Falcon Lodge they had many interesting and varied reminiscences to convey.

Deborah Shorey.

I was just twenty when I got married. My husband had joined the army at Christmas. We were going to get married on his first leave and so he came home in April. He had five days. We went to the Registry Office to get the licence to get married, but as I was only 20 they wouldn't let me, as I needed my Father's permission as I had to be 21.

I had to wait three days for the certificate to come through. My husband was stationed over in Ireland and I went over to see him. There were a lot of troops there and wherever we went we had to carry our gasmasks and tin hats.

Where we lived in Sutton we could see the bombing of Coventry at night. I was working in Erdington at that time. One day I went to Erdington to work and it had been bombed. Erdington was a very popular place for the Germans to bomb because of its munition factories. That morning every shop front was lying on the pavement. You couldn't walk up the High Street, as there was glass everywhere.

It was the time of the landmines and one morning when we came out to go to work, landmines had been dropped during the night and all over the ground were the roofs of houses. There were no houses whatsoever, but there was this bottle of milk standing on the pavement! It had been missed!

I worked on the electrical wiring for the Spitfires. It was a new experience for me as we were country girls and had no experience of factory life. We thought it was funny when the factory girls were trying to teach us. Half a dozen were factory girls and the rest of us were newcomers.

Two land army girls lived with my sister and we would go there for some extra eggs as they worked on the poultry farm. Everyone was friendly and would help everyone else.

I lived in Slade Road, Roughley, and as the German bombers were returning from a raid sometimes they would drop one or two bombs. They dropped them in the field just down the road where I lived. The dents from the bombs have been in that field until just now when they built new houses. The farmer used to just put the cattle on them and did not take any notice.

Mrs Winn.

It so happened that my husband was working in Coventry and he was coming home to my house on Shepherd's Green Road, in Erdington. He had a friend who had a motorbike with a sidecar. Because of the blackout they couldn't have any headlights on so they had a little torch and it lit the way for them all the way from Coventry to Birmingham.

They were nearing home and bombers were coming over. I was sitting in the shelter with my baby and little girl. There was a German plane overhead. We heard some one in the garden and it was our next door neighbour. He had taken a drink and was full of humour! He was wearing a colander on his head, as he couldn't find his tin hat! So you see, you had lots of fun as well.

Then this lady came up with her little boy. She had dragged him all the way along the road and he was saying, "Aunty, I can't walk anymore. She's put both of my legs down one leg of my trousers!"

The first road that was bombed was the second road along from us. We were in bed. It was terrible. About twenty houses were hit and there were people killed as well.

Doris Bonsall.

I lived in Neville Road, Erdington. There was black stuff on the window. It was really horrible. We were lucky as we had our own shelter. During a raid we would take all our things down there.

We were lucky, really lucky, as a bomb landed on the next road, George Road, and killed some people there. It shook the whole house. I had all the animals in with me, in the shelter, cats and dogs. There was my husband, two dogs, two cats and myself.

There was one time when I went down the shelter with my daughter in a carrycot. When we came up the next morning, people said, "What have you been doing down there all night?"

I replied, "Well, the sirens went."

"But that was the All Clear" they said! We had gone down on the All Clear. I must have been in the house during the raid and then got up when I heard the All Clear. I used to sleep heavily in those days.

We went on holiday to Aberystwyth. Our relatives there used go for miles in the car to see where a bomb had dropped in the country. My husband's brother once went to London to watch an air raid! When he saw one he didn't want to see any more. There was us thinking, isn't it lovely to have a few nights without air raids? They didn't realise how awful it was until they had gone through it.

When I stayed at his Mother's in Wales I could not believe it. She would send me to the little shop for a pound of butter and due to the rationing we were only allowed two ounces. I stood outside the shop. I waited until everyone had gone out before going in. The shopkeeper said, "What would you like?"

It was amazing as we were so rationed at home. Little bits of this and that, but in Wales you could have anything you wanted. They would come round from the farms with baskets of eggs. It didn't seem right to us, as we had nothing really.

Joan Daniels.

During the war I lived in a village called Moira which is near Burton-Upon Trent. Life was almost normal for me except for the blackouts. It was tedious I suppose looking back. Get up in the morning; go to work and come home. I travelled daily on the train and if the sirens went off, the train would stop and you just stood there until the All Clear went.

At the weekends, a group of six of us, who all had cycles, would cycle into the countryside. We would have something to eat and drink at a country pub and then get the old legs going again. It was great fun; weekends were really enjoyable as we cycled for miles. When I got home soaked to the skin after a storm once, mother came out with a bowl of hot water and mustard. She got me to put my feet in the hot water and the sun came out, blazing gloriously about nine o'clock at night. That lives in my memory. We had some marvellous times.

I met my husband at the firm I worked for. His name was Doug. We didn't work in the same office but I knew him before the war. Moira was a famous colliery and our firm did the accounts. He came over to do the accounts. I happened to say to him one day, "What do you with yourself at lunchtime?"

He replied, "I take sandwiches."

I said, "Would you like to take a walk up to my house?" I was just being sociable, so he took his sandwiches to my house and had a cup of tea and had a chat with my mother and sister.

At the end of the audit my mother and sister got a present from Doug's Mother. I didn't get one and I was most indignant.

"I do declare," I said, "I arrange all this and you get presents and I get nothing."

Then about a week after, I came home and said, "Mom, I've got my present. Doug has asked me to go to the pictures with him. Can I go?"

I was seventeen but you used to have to ask your Mother's permission.

"I don't know about that." She said.

"Come on," I replied, "You got your present what about me?"

"Well, I don't suppose he will ask you again."

"I don't suppose he will."

"Well then you can go."

But he did ask me again and that's how it all began. Just twelve months after that he was called up into the forces and he went to India. His eyesight prevented him from joining the Aircrew so he worked in accounts. He became Aircraftman H.D. Daniels and his number was 1295701. He rose to the rank of sergeant.

We wrote to each other and in that way we kept in touch. When he was in India he told me that the letters he received made him very happy, as he could almost know what was happening back in England, as they were so descriptive.

When he got home he rang me where I worked. Someone in the office said there was a phone call for me and a voice said, "Remember me?" and I knew straight away who it was. Instead of going home that night I went on the train to Rolleston and there he was standing on the platform all in his uniform.

Aircraftman H.D. Daniels, (back row top left wearing glasses) later Sergeant Daniels, with colleagues in India. Sergeant Daniels described the scene as 'The Happy Family.'

Indian soldier, Isaiah Singh taken by Sergeant Daniels, in India.

Sergeant Daniels, (front row, extreme right, wearing sunglasses) with colleagues at Indian border.

War was declared on the 3rd of September 1939. Most of the country could be found huddled around wirelesses listening to the sombre and solemn words of the Prime Minister, Neville Chamberlain. The United Kingdom had a Tripartite agreement with France and Poland that if any one of them were to be invaded the other two would immediately come to their aid.

I have been to Poland and heard great stories of the Polish resistance. In Warsaw where I stayed I could not help but notice that there were flowers and lit candles forming little shrines on many street corners. These were in memory of the many Polish people who were indiscriminately taken from their homes and shot by the Nazis. Local people always decorate with flowers the city's sculpture, that pays tribute to the Warsaw Uprising in April 1943. 60, 000 Poles were killed in the fighting or sent to death camps.

I went to the site of the famous Jewish ghetto. By December 1941 200,000 people were crammed into the disease ridden ghetto with scarce shelter and food. I stood where the trains came in June 1941 and carried whole families off to the concentration camp at Triblinka.

I saw the remains of a track from a German Panzer tank that had been left embedded in the cathedral wall. Such was Hitler's hate of the Polish people that he ordered the city to be razed to the ground before the advancing Russians could arrive.

I was also aware of the heroic deeds of the Polish airmen stationed in England during the war. There was a squadron based at Castle Bromwich Airfield, and as the Polish pilots were very experienced, they used to test - fly the planes. I came across Janek Piela, a resident of Birmingham but a native of Poland, who had some rather fascinating memories to tell.

Janek Piela a resident of Moseley.

I come from the West of Poland, from a small village called Adamowice. In 1939 I was a volunteer in the Polish Air Force which was situated in Warsaw. I was in the airforce band, playing the trumpet, and of course I didn't expect the war when it started on the first of September 1939. At the time we were supposed to be helping the firemen, as they were expecting some fires. Then a German bomber came on the 3rd of September and they started bombing the airport in Warsaw. I had a lucky escape there; a bomb came falling towards me as I went running towards the fire station. The bomb landed not very far away and some glass came down and I had a few scratches on my back and neck.

We were evacuated from Warsaw to a small town on the outskirts of Warsaw. Eventually we were shifted towards the East and we were packed on a train, which was supposed to go towards the Russian border.

At the time I was on the train, there were still German aeroplanes bombing and I thought that I would be lucky if I was still alive the next day. Nearly every day you didn't know if you would live, or die, you just followed the orders and hoped for the best.

The train stopped because we were told that the Russians were occupying the towns in front so we had to leave the train. We were about hundred kilometres away from Warsaw.

From there, we were supposed to join a Polish unit somewhere in a village. Well I was only young, I was about 18/19 and of course everything was upside down for me. We landed in a small village surrounded by Germans. The whole village was bombed and shelled and houses were on fire as shells were exploding everywhere. Everybody was running away from the village.

Then, I was captured by the German Army. The shirt and trousers I was wearing were from the Polish Air Force. They were asking me this and that and eventually I had to tell them that I was in the army, and then a German Sergeant pulled a pistol and put it against my temple and he said, 'You are lying to me.' You don't lie when they pull a pistol on you.

As a POW, I was shifted from one place to the other. I had to march, travel by lorry and by train; eventually I landed up in Prussia in North Germany.

They put me in a camp. Eventually I was allowed to go to a German farm and to help on the farm and I was there for a couple of years. Well I was quite happy there, I liked a bit of farming, as we had a small farm at home so I knew all about it and I had plenty of food. The farmer liked me; he wasn't married, he was living with his sister and his parents who were still alive. I was quite able to speak to him as I spoke German as well as Polish. While I was there I learned how to speak German much better. He told me that he was in the First World War and he was in the artillery, with the horses pulling the cannons.

My dad made an application that I shouldn't be a Prisoner of War, as I came from Silesia, which was near the German border and that my dad had fought in the First World War in the German army. Secondly the Germans had citizen lists. German list Number 1 was a perfect German, number 2, 3 and 4 were Polish people.

Because of the above, I was on the number two list. They were then able to free me from the POW camp.

Then I went home and I learned how to drive a lorry, as there were a lot of demands for lorry divers. I applied to drive a lorry. Eventually, all the young men from Silesia as far as I know had to join the German army. So after a year being at home I had to join the German army. I drove ambulances at first.

I was in the anti aircraft unit as a driver and we were sent right up to the Russian front towards St Petersburg. You could see some of the train engines all blown up and whole trains lying on their sides. The Russians were pushing the German army back and I was sent to Leningrad, which is St Petersburg now. The Germans were retreating but our unit was still going forward. The other German soldiers would all laugh at us and say, you had better turn around and go back home.

When we got off the train I was welcomed by shells and soldiers shooting at us.

The roads were very bad; they were all sandy and went over hills. Where it was muddy they put planks and it was very slippery, there was a load of lorries slipping off the track into a big ditch. It was very bad everywhere. And of course everywhere we went was destroyed, the towns and villages were all burned out already. I think it was 1944, so for four years the Germans were advancing and destroying everything.

I was the only one from my unit and the whole company, which was about 200, who spoke Polish and of course anybody who spoke Polish could more or less understand the Russians. I was very interested in speaking the Russian language, to get to know the Russian girls.

If we needed some help in the kitchen, they used to send for me to get some young girls, to peel the potatoes and do the washing up. The girls were quite happy to help as they welcomed the Germans. But there was a lot of Russian people who didn't like us coming at all. They had the jitters as the German army was coming to invade and then afterwards all the villages were gutted. Plus there was a lot of resentment for taking over their villages and taking whatever they wanted. Also we went sometimes where there were no Germans in the village and you could see that all the men ran away from the village to hide.

I was away from my family for three years. I was driving the lorry, which combined, as a kitchen. I was a driver but I also had to help in the kitchen.

Once, we got stuck in the mud and Russian tanks were shooting at us and we had to abandon the lorry. Everybody was running away. As there was a train near by we tried to get on that train. That was the last train on that track and Russian tanks surrounded us but luckily everybody managed to get on the train. We travelled from Russia towards Lithuania; the train destroyed the track while we were still on it. It was pulling the track up. There was a big hook on the back of the train and as we went along it broke up the entire track.

I landed up near the capital of Lithuania. I found my unit again and we were sent to West Germany, somewhere near Luxembourg. Anyway they gave us new equipment and new lorries and they sent us back to fight the Americans. The Battle of the Bulge took place there. We were there to push the Americans back. But I was just driving so I wasn't at the front but we went so many kilometres forward that we took some Americans as Prisoners of War.

But everything went wrong afterwards. We had to move back and my unit was smashed as there were bombings going on all the time. A friend and I decided it was time to depart from the German army and we gave ourselves up.

So we gave ourselves up as Prisoners of War and were taken by the Americans in their jeeps. They took us to a railway station, where there was a lot of German soldiers being looked after as Prisoners of War.

The Americans eventually transported us to Cherbourg, which is a French town on the coast. I was separated from the others as I was Polish and if I wanted to, I could join a Polish unit in England. We could join the Polish army in England, to fight the Germans!

So I joined the Polish army and we were transported by boat to Southampton, then from Southampton we travelled up north to Scotland.

We were equipped with an English uniform. We were then sent to the camp at Catterick. I had to learn how to drive tanks. I just had a few lessons when the war had finished so I never finished the course.

So the war was finished and we were asked if we wanted to stay in England, there was plenty of work. Or we just put our names on the list and to go back to where we had come from. As it happens I was a bit of a musician so I thought, 'Oh well I might as well try my luck up here as a musician.'

But I had to take some job as a handy man on a building site and from Scotland I was sent down to Birmingham and I landed another job on a building site. Eventually, I found some friends and we had enough people to make a Polish band and that's how I started playing in Polish bands. I made my life here in Birmingham and have lived here ever since.

I found it fascinating to discover that when the Germans attacked Moscow in December 1941, under Operation Barbarossa, a few German patrols reached a tram terminus in one of the suburbs of Moscow. The soldiers could see the dome of St Basil's shining in the winter sun. It would be like German soldiers reaching the old bus terminus at the Yenton in Erdington!

Janek Piela in German uniform after serving in the Polish Airforce.

Jan was in three different forces. The Polish Airforce, the German Army and the Polish Free Army!

Janek and German soldiers practising. Janek's older brother, George is the one holding the machine gun.

64

Thomas Paine resident of Sutton Coldfield.

My father worked at a pawnbroker on the corner of Grosvenor Road, Aston, (later to become Sparrows the greengrocers). I lived in Wyrley Road with my mother and three sisters and I was born there in 1934. Within a few weeks of me being born my parents decided to move and open up a men's outfitting shop in Lichfield Road Aston, opposite the Britannia Pub. This was where my fourth sister was born.

Us children all went to Aston Hall School and we all in turn went through the infants and junior parts but with the coming of the war in 1939 our parents decided that we should move further out, for safety I presume; though truth was it wasn't much safer. We moved to Frances Road Erdington, but we continued our schooling in Aston. My three older sisters went to Victoria Road School later on, while my mother looked after the shop and my father was directed to work at the GEC Wilton as a clerk.

Around the end of the thirties I can remember being taken for the day out to Castle Bromwich Aerodrome, where the biplanes were used for training, (I've always been interested in aircraft.) Little did we know that over half the spitfires built would be built over the road from the Aerodrome. Later on I was to discover that someone I knew very well assembled spitfires there.

One of the amusing things that happened to us as children, was when we were issued with gas masks and my younger sister and I had what were called Mickey Mouse masks, which were blue and red with silver rims around the eye pieces. For devilment we would chase each other around wearing them. They used to make your face sweat like mad.

My father dug a hole about six feet deep in our back garden and installed an Anderson shelter, the soil from the hole being put over the top together with sandbags for further protection. It had bunks fitted in side and a sort of porch over the entrance, with a raised step to stop it filling up with water when it rained. The only thing is that after being in the shelter for a few hours you got a lot of condensation dripping onto you from the roof and you could get quite wet. As the war progressed and our forces were on the offensive, hence no more bombing, the shelter was mainly used to play in.

My father joined the ARP and became a section leader. So we didn't see him much when the raids were on. He was also a member of the St John's

Ambulance Brigade, so he must have been very busy and he used to keep us informed about the bomb damage next morning. There were a lot of prime targets around Erdington and Aston, the GEC, ICI Kynocks, Dunlop, and the rail sheds.

I remember very well my father taking me to see some friends in Coventry within a few days of the biggest raid and seeing the terrible devastation.

I also remember going to school one morning and seeing the terrible bombing around the Queens Road area of Aston. Hardly anything was left standing. Some of my friends lived there, but luckily they survived. We were told most of the damage was caused by land mines. The war was an exciting time for us lads and needless to say we were always playing soldiers especially anywhere there was a bombsite.

During the latter part of the war my mother became part of the Hospitality Committee. This was set up to give billeting in private houses for foreign troops. The headquarters of this was somewhere around the Hall of Memory.

We had troops of all nationalities, Canadian, Belgium, American and at least one Czechoslovakian, who was very withdrawn and didn't communicate very much. For the most part though they were very nice people and one of the Belgians kept in touch with our family well into the 1960's. At that time he had become a police officer.

My father was very friendly with a black American, who after the war sent him a copy of the book 'The Rights of Man' by Thomas Paine, which we still have and an Canadian airman bought me a Monopoly board game, the first I'd ever seen. Most of them spoilt us kids. I suppose because most of them were missing their own children.

Towards the end of the war, my eldest sister left school and went to work at the Wolsely Sheep Shearing Company in Wilton, making ammunition. When the war ended my two eldest sisters used to go to town dancing and met some young English soldiers from Leicester. My eldest sister married one of them in March 1947, this young soldier in the Royal Artillery had spend four years in a Prisoner of War Camp in Germany, after being captured in the desert when the British were retreating. Needless to say he became a hero to me.

At the end of the war when fathers of my friends came home quite a few souvenirs were given to us kids. I remember being in possession of a Lugar pistol and an American army bayonet. We didn't keep these things long, we were forever swapping them for what we thought was a better bargain, cigarette cards and Dinky toys etc.

In early May of this year I was very privileged to be invited to the HOLOCAUST COMMEMORATION at Witton Cemetery by the Council of Birmingham and Midland Jewry. It was a very moving service and a poignant reminder of the immense suffering that was inflicted on the Jewish people during the Second World War.

Heinrich Himmler, Chief of the SS was responsible for the transportation and death of millions of Jews. It was Himmler who approved and carried out the "Final Solution." It was part of Hitler's "New Order." In reality millions of Jews were massacred in the death camps in East Europe as part of the Nazis pernicious and perverted racial policies.

Some weeks after the Commemoration I was invited to interview members of Birmingham's Jewish Community who had memories of the war. The first one listed, is given by Lionel Singer, who is Chairman of the Birmingham and Midland Jewry. The interviews were later given to me by members of the Birmingham Jewish Ex-Servicemen and Women's Association.

Lionel Singer.

I would like to tell you a bit about my paternal back ground. My grandfather came from a town in Russia called Chernigov. He frequently travelled from Russia to the port of Hull bringing over horses on behalf of traders, these having been sold, he would return to Russia.

Eventually, he decided to settle in England and sent for his wife, Anne and children to join him. At the time my grandmother was pregnant with my father. Unfortunately my grandmother gave birth whilst still at sea and as the boat was on international waters, he was (that is my father) regarded as stateless and remained so for the rest of his life.

This state of affairs was of no great significance until the outbreak of the Second World War in 1939, (although I must point out that my father had served in the British army during the First World War). Unfortunately on the outbreak of the Second World War, being legally stateless, he was regarded as an alien and was required to register with the police. This situation remained throughout the war even to the extent of having to inform the authorities if he intended to leave the city for any reason.

We as children considered my grandmother, Anne, as a little eccentric. The reason for this was explained as follows: During one of many attacks on her village, Steradof, by Cossacks during their frequent pogroms, she was slashed across the face with a sabre, the scars from which she carried all her life.

At the outbreak of war in 1939, I was eleven. My background is that I was born in London. Number 2 Pitfirst Street, Hoxton, next to the baths.

My father was a tailor and work had been difficult to find in Birmingham. He cycled to London and found some temporary work as a tailor. My mother joined him. In consequence I was born in London. Shortly after I was born we moved back to Birmingham. Round about 1930 we moved to Ladywood. We lived there until we were bombed out in 1941.

The day war was declared, September the 3rd 1939 was a Sunday. I remember standing in the street, slightly bewildered about what was going on around me. I was listening to the wireless when the announcement by Neville Chamberlain was made saying that this country was now at war.

I wasn't even quite sure what that meant, but what it did mean was that the school that I was attending which was the Birmingham Hebrew School, in St Luke's Road was going to be evacuated. The school was evacuated to Coalville in Leicester.

By this time my elder brother had been moved from Birmingham, with his company. He worked for the Odeon Cinemas. He moved lock stock and barrel down to Marlow near London. So the only two left at home was my sister and myself and for whatever the reason we were not evacuated with the school. Consequently our schooling was interrupted. So from September 3rd 1939 my formal education virtually ceased. Though there was some schooling offered in one room of the school for the few children that were left. By and large we went when it pleased us, or not as the case may be.

Generally speaking the war seemed fairly quiet until round about May

1940, when the Germans invaded the Low Countries and France. It was at this time when the first air raid started. Life changed completely. It became one round of getting up in the morning, going to school for an hour or two coming home and then round about six o'clock packing up all our bedding and making for the shelters. We endured this night after night, for something like six months. There were constant air raids day and night.

Unfortunately we were bombed and our house was destroyed and several people, who lived in and round the area, including our old friend who managed the Dolphin pub in Irving Street, were killed that night. I think his name was Jesse Watton.

We were then moved by the council to 39 Gough Road and there we settled in to a life of slightly fewer air raids but of worsening war news and tighter rationing. We were told daily of defeat, in North Africa, Greece and wherever the fighting was taking place. The news seemed to get worse by the day, and with the sinking of ships rationing became more severe.

As I mentioned the school was evacuated, because of the fear of air raids. Not only were school children evacuated but also several people from the community took themselves to various outskirts of Birmingham and other cities.

The life of the Jewish community in Birmingham was interrupted. The Services and the whole Jewish way of life were in turmoil. However it settled down during the war. The blackouts of course affected the lighting of the Synagogues so all times of services had to be changed to conform to the blackout regulations. The Synagogues were too large to be blacked out.

Another thing that happened to the Jewish community, was the influx of Jewish service men from around the world. Polish, Czechs, Austrian all sorts of nationalities created an international flavour. They made their way to Birmingham for services, Kosher meals and to make use of the few shops that were available. This was an interesting time for me.

When the Americans arrived, anyone who was lucky enough to entertain them not only entertained the American servicemen, but also entertained the bags of goodies that they were likely to bring. They brought foodstuff that we hadn't seen in two/three years. Butter, sugar, eggs, chocolate.

One of the Americans was a man called, Robert Beck. His visits became very regular, when we realised that he had an ulterior motive and that was my sister. In the fullness of time Robert Beck married my sister, Jean Singer in1944 and fifty odd years later they are still happily married living in the United States.

Questions are being asked constantly, about what information was coming over regarding the Jews of Europe. As a child my first experience was when we met refugees who were coming into the country in 1938/39. I didn't really understand the reason for them coming. We saw all these young children dressed in their continental clothes, totally different from us.

And slowly the news came of what was happening in Germany. To a simple child's mind, Jews were being brutalised and forced out of their country having to leave their parents behind. To my regret though, we didn't show enough sympathy and understanding of their plight.

Maybe, it was difficult to understand the scale of what was happening in Europe and Germany and the brutalities that went with it.

Throughout the war, there were meetings at various Jewish halls, where speakers who had escaped from Germany had information and would try to disseminate what they had heard and in some instances what they had actually seen and experienced. I think most people found it incomprehensible that a civilised country like Germany could be persecuting Jews. People found it very difficult to understand and there was a suggestion that some of these claims had been made up. Gradually after the war and of course tragically it eventually unfolded that these stories where found to be true.

And with great bitterness now, we recall the pleas for help, the pleas to let in more adults and children. We remember the embargo on Jews escaping to Palestine and the difficulties that were put in the way, by the British government who had a mandate over Palestine. With their constant refusal to allow Jews in over the prescribed number. Thereby consigning them to the death camps.

Thinking about the war in general, of course it wasn't totally depressing. The war from time to time was a happy event. In retrospect the two most significant occasions were the shifting of the ban of the ringing of church bells. After 1940 they were only to be rung in an event of an invasion. That embargo was lifted after the victory at El Alamein and the ringing of the church bells heralded the first real victory that Britain had experienced. Indeed we now realise that was the turning point of the whole war.

The other personal significant occasion was the day my sister was married at the Singers Hill Synagogue in Birmingham, to Robert Beck, who was a Corporal in the American Army. The Americans were always known for their generosity. They arrived with eggs, sugar, and butter, things that we had forgotten existed. All these, prior to the wedding were put together to produce the most beautiful and luxurious cake, that you had ever wished to see, oozing with all the luxuries that we hadn't seen and never thought we would see again. If I don't remember the wedding, I certainly remember the wedding cake! I also remember a jeep baring the name 'Little Jean', that was the name of my sister.

Arthur Chesses.

I was born in Handsworth, Birmingham. I had only eaten kosher food and it was quite a shock to me to have to get used to army food. One of the first meals I was given was bully beef, I ate it of course, but I was really sick. It was a strange feeling, but you had to get used to it and I thought I would do it the hard way.

I journeyed from Carlisle up to Stranrear, then from there across to Larne. And I finished up in Omagh. There was a very big army depot which was for the three regiments, the Inneskilen Fusiliers, the Royal Irish Fusiliers and the unit I was in, the Royal Ulster Rifles.

We were very young and very innocent and we knew very little about Irish history. I couldn't understand why we were confined to camp, on a particular day until it was explained to me the reason why. It was the guys from the Free State, Eire, who had joined the British Army and they explained all about the troubles in Ireland.

The men from the Free State used to go home on leave. They wore suits, as they were not allowed to go home in uniform.

We used to have a religious service there. I found a guy there who I knew at school; he was in the Inneskilen Fusiliers and a few of us got together and we used to have a little Jewish service. At that particular camp I didn't see a Jewish padre. One of us would take over; who knew a bit about it. I was pretty well up on Hebrew, so we were able to have a little service, which was very nice. It brought us together a bit.

I do remember going to Belfast for weekends leave. And I felt that there would be Jews in Belfast. I went to a Jewish club there. I think it was called Bell Vue, if I remember rightly.

I did not experience any Anti-Semitism throughout all the years that I was in the Army, which was over four, and a half. I think it was because we were all doing the same thing. That we all had our problems and religion didn't really come into it.

When I was stationed in Germany there was a special Passover service, which had been specially arranged for Jews, from all over Germany. I wasn't going to go, and my Officer who was quite a religious man, said that I ought to go. He put it in such a way that I might be in trouble if I didn't.

I wasn't really aware what was happening to the Jews in Germany. After the war was over I was horrified when I found out.

About six weeks after D-Day, I landed in Normandy. My unit was the Royal Scots. I went to Montgomery's head quarters, as I was Infantry attached and we had to guard the big people there. We used to see 'Monty' fairly often. The HQ was always full of Generals, Brigadiers and all sorts. Bad-Ounhausen was the name of Monty's HQ. I was there until the end of the of the war.

At that time I was nineteen and a half going on twenty. The war was over then and we were attached to the Royal Engineers, who were responsible for the bridges that had been destroyed. I was attached to them as infantry.

Germany was destroyed! It was unbelievable the result of some of the bombing. I went to Hanover, and whatever the bombing that happened in this country was nothing compared to what we had done. It is magnificent how they built it all up again after the war, after we had knocked it to bits.

It was a dreadful shock when I realised what had happened to the Jews in the war.

I don't talk about it much.

I feel anger to this day, to the Germans. I don't take it to the extreme, but it is very hard. Whenever I see the films and I see thousands and thousands of people with their arms up, shouting' Heil Hitler'. I often think, 'Where did they all go?' Because at the end of the war, whenever I spoke to anybody, they never had anything to do with Hitler. I don't like to be racist, but I don't like losing to the Germans, even at football.

Obviously a happy time was when the war was actually over and I had settled in billets in Germany. One of my happiest times was my first leave. I was stationed in Brussels for a while. We were clearing out German billets that they had taken over in Brussels. And I came across this Jewish prayer book. I still have it and the next time I go to Israel I am going to take it with me and I am going to present it to the Holocaust Museum.

Jeanette Franklin.

I was born in Birmingham and was fourteen years old and going to Grammar School when the war broke out. I left school and went to typing college and at sixteen got a job doing shorthand typing. It was boring and I hated it. I wanted to do something exciting and get away from home. I persuaded my parents to lie about my age so I could join the army. They did so reluctantly.

My basic army training started at Wrexham, and we could choose our jobs. There were cooks, office personnel and drivers. I wanted radiolocation. I didn't have a clue what it was, knew nothing about it, but just felt it would be exciting – and it was.

I was fortunate to get accepted, and was sent to Oswestry with several other girls from Birmingham, where we had our basic training on radiolocation (which Radar was then called). After we passed our exams we were formed into an Artillery Regiment, (known as 'Ack Ack') which consisted of four batteries, each split into two units, making eight gun sights to be manned.

Radar consisted of two cabins, which had aerials protruding from the side and the top. These had to be maintained and kept free from grease, and to do this we had to climb a perpendicular ladder up to the top aerials and as the equipment was on high ground anyway this was more terrifying.

The clothes we originally wore consisted of men's battle-dress and overcoats, and it was two or three months before we had uniforms suitable for women.

From Oswestry, (now as a complete regiment) we were sent to a place called Weybourne, which was extremely bleak and cold. There was no running water in this camp; in fact the only things running were rats and mice. We went on duty wearing battle dress, gaiters, boots, jerkins and overcoats all at once. (Were we really on the East Coast?) The food was awful, so we filled up on 'pink cakes' from the NAAFI and we all put weight on.

As I mentioned before, Weybourne was a trainee firing camp and we trained on a 'sleeve'. This was trailed from an aeroplane, and we had to shoot at it! Although the 'sleeve' was a distance away from the plane I think the pilots were either very brave or very stupid.

After Weybourne the serious part of our job began. We were sent to Derby and the gun site was on the racecourse, situated near the town. The German bombs had not reached that far then, so we did not see any action. We spent our time getting used to the equipment and each other. There had been a lot of jealously from other instrument operators (i.e. Predictor operators) regarding Radar. This was because we were top secret and no one else was allowed in our area. Eventually we all got to know each other and petty feelings were soon forgotten, and we all worked as a team, who were all men (lucky us!) There was no strong discipline in our unit, unlike some. This was because we had a very good C.O who realised he could get more out of us by being liberal. As we found to our relief one-day, when we were so cold and we did not have any fuel for our stoves. So some of us decided to creep onto the racecourse and chop down a few trees and hedges for firewood. Suffice to say we were found out and put on a civil charge. However, our liberal C.O and a female officer managed to get the charge dropped. It was not always hard work and we managed to have a few laughs and a few dances in the mess hall.

From Derby, we were sent back to the East Coast – this time to a gun site near Great Yarmouth. There was plenty of action there, and we had to get used to the noise from the 3.7 artillery gun being fired, up to twenty-four hours a day. Our sleeping huts were situated a few yards from these monsters, and our rickety bunk beds would sway from side to side, but like everything else we got used to the noise. One funny, or not so funny, incident happened one morning as we were dressing in our denim overalls, which we wore for maintenance work. One of the girls suddenly started screaming, and then we all started screaming, why? We saw a huge black beetle crawling up her overalls. One brave soul managed to knock it off (not me) and we all agreed the guns were less frightening.

Next to our gun site in Yarmouth was a searchlight battery and the enemy planes would fire down the beam of the searchlight. Occasionally when we were running up the 'cat walk' to our equipment, the enemy machine gunning was too near for comfort, and one girl was unfortunately killed.

Our next gun site was at Cleethorps (again the East Coast). Again, we did not see very much action, but experienced excitement in other ways. This part of the East Coast was allegedly strong 5th Column. The 5th Column was men and women who were sympathetic to Germany and spied for them. One incident stands out, because it involved two friends and myself. We went to Cleethorps for our half-day out, and made our way to our favourite café. Which was built into a huge rock called the Grotto. Sitting at our usual table by the window, we realised for the third time we had sat there we could hear Morse code. Not understanding Morse code we decided to report it to our C.O. The next week we went to the café, and found it closed. We never got to the bottom of why it was, but to this day we would like to think we played a part in closing down a 5th Column spy ring, as did happen to two of my friends who were also in my Radar team.

My friends sometimes used to go to another tearoom in Grimsby. There they became quite friendly with a vicar who eventually invited them to the Vicarage for tea, at least twice. They became suspicious of him when he started to ask too may personal questions about their work, their battery and army life in general. They reported him to their C.O and later on a government man was sent to debrief them. They were told to go back to the Vicarage when invited, which happened a few days later. A trap was set, the Vicar was duly arrested and the girls were sworn to secrecy, at least until the war was over.

After spending three years moving up and down the East Coast, we went for a while to the South Coast. This was where we experienced our first 'Buzz Bombs'. At the same time more cities up North were being bombarded so we were sent back to the East Coast. My time in the army was exciting and at times very scary. I feel proud to have served in the way I did, and I made some life-long friends.

We were never really aware what was taking place in Central Europe as very little news filtered through to us. We heard either by an occasional radio or a trip to the cinema, due to the remote locations of our gun site. We caught up with the news when on leave.

My last move was to South Shields where our activity had stopped due to the war coming to a close. The excitement of V.E day passed us by unfortunately, as the news did not filter through very quickly.

Being Jewish did not affect me in any way, I did not experience Anti-Semitism, and I either ate the food or starved. We were all too busy trying to win the war, and a great camaraderie existed between our batteries regardless of race, colour or creed.

Jan, also known as Ginger was in the Ack Ack as was Violet Horsley. I remember as a child my Mother telling me stories of the, "Girls in Hyde Park" who used to man the guns. She used to pass them on the bus, as she was a "Clippie," otherwise known as a bus conductress.

*Jeanette "Ginger" Franklin
in ATS uniform.*

Ginger and colleagues ready to ride off!
The girls in the picutre are Vicky, Ginger, Cath, Jess and Hilda.

To Ginger - love Jim.
Friendships and relationships were severed during the war. Photographs, post-cards and letters were often the only means of keeping friendships, as there was great uncertainty to when one would meet again.

Arnold Wilks.

I was born in London and came to Birmingham when I was ten and a half. I am now eighty years old.

In 1939 conscription came in. I was nineteen at the time and like most of the Jewish boys in Birmingham of that age, we were all joining the Territorial Army.

My father was in the artillery during the First World War, so I naturally gravitated towards the artillery unit. The unit I joined started in Stechford and it was an off shoot of the territorial unit in Stony Lane, Sparkhill.

I was working at the time in the offices in Lucas in Great Hampton Street and we had to go away for the annual Territorial camp, that was a must. Needless to say my first meal when I was at territorial camp was a piece of bacon, with maybe an egg or a sausage on the plate. But when I looked at it, it made me think that I had only eaten kosher food at home and I thought well, I have to eat something, so I ate it. I never worried then.

Whilst we were there, war broke out. We were given forty eight hours leave, to settle our affairs and after that we were sent up to Stranraer. I caught a boat to Larne, and I was violently sick all the way. First time I had been on a boat outside Cannon Hill Park!
It was a terrible experience.

We landed in Ireland and we went to a place called Ballymoney. I served in a lot of different towns in Ireland. Eventually I was posted to a Yorkshire unit and I joined them in Rye, Sussex. It was a very good unit and I was very happy there. I wasn't very happy in my previous unit I had been in. Not through any anti – Semitism or anything like that, I just wasn't very happy there.

We moved around a bit and eventually we ended up in Aldershot. I then went up to Liverpool, passing through Birmingham funnily enough. We caught the boat from Liverpool and sailed on Christmas Day 1942 and landed in Algiers. We then drove through the Atlas Mountains. We were there to advance towards Egypt as the Eighth Army advanced towards Algiers. I remember seeing hundreds and thousands of Germans troops but the Eighth Army then went over to Sicily. We leap frogged over them and we landed in Salerno. It was about two days after the original landing and the place was still burning. In typical army fashion our guns were landed on a different beach so we messed about for the day on the beach as it was being shelled. Nevertheless we took no notice and we went swimming because it was very hot, terribly hot.

There was a sunken ship out at sea, and a couple of us swam out to this sunken ship and climbed on board and had a look around. We didn't find anything, a lot of broken glass and paper and stuff but I was game for anything!

Before Italy we were in a place called Sedjaine, which is in North Africa. We lobbed a few over to the Germans and they lobbed a few back, and every body settled down for the rest of the day. Nothing dramatic happened.

The spotter plane used to come over every day at the same time. We had a terrible tropical storm one night and the whole place turned into a quagmire of mud, really terrible. The gun towing vehicles could not get in to tow the guns out. So we were told to spike the guns, this means that you put a shell down one end and a shell up the other end and you fire, and it splits the barrel which means the guns are of no use. Then we had to get out.

The next day we were in a wood and we were told that there were lorries of German infantry coming down. I remember setting myself up on a bend in the road, with a Bren gun, and sitting there priming a box of hand-grenades. But luckily nothing happened and we were told to mount up and off we went. Eventually after some time we got new guns and we then carried on to various places in North Africa.

After the landing in Salerno in Italy, we went right up through Salerno on the West Coast and through the centre of Italy. It is a very mountainous country. I voluntarily transferred to a unit called the Counter Mortar Section, although I was still attached to my own regiment. I was trained to use the radio, compass, and maps. I looked out for any enemy action and this meant tanks, artillery flashes, troop movement, lorries, anything. I would take a compass bearing and radio it back, so the command post could bring down whatever he liked, planes, artillery fire, whatever.

I remember seeing a most terrific tank battle, from the top of a hill where I was hiding. That was a sight to be seen. It was in Italy. I had never seen anything like it before. It was a load of tanks going at each other with a lot of them on fire, burning up.

We used to dress how we wanted to and we had our own cook and just one officer. It was a small compact unit. The first time I remember doing the job, it was evening and everybody of course wanted to be the first one up to try this out. Anyway, my Officer said to me, "Wilks, you!" So we went up this mountain with the infantry boys. We got to the top of this mountain and we couldn't dig in because it was basically rock, so we just hid behind some bushes. Then we found that we couldn't get any information back to base to the command post because something has gone wrong with the radio. We couldn't tune it in at all. So we got the BBC on and we sat there listening to the news from London!

No rations came up for us of course and I remember the next morning walking along the top of this mountain and there was an officer sitting on the edge of a slit trench, swinging his legs and I said, "Good morning Sir."

And he said, "Bloody lovely war, isn't it?" I asked him if he had anything to eat as we hadn't got anything and he said, 'I can give you a packet of biscuits'.

Eventually they came up for us with the jeep and they took us back. That was my first experience on the Counter Mortar.

Another time was that we were on the top of this hill, another chap and me. There was a cave, so obviously we moved into the cave because it was safer.

We used to go and do a stint on the edge of the hill, to do some spotting. Well we were going to make some breakfast. We had condensed cubes of porridge and powdered milk that you mix with water and we lit a fire in the cave but we didn't realise that the smoke was going outside. There was a tree just outside the cave and I had put my very good great coat and a small pack with everything in it against this tree.

Well, the Germans must have spotted the smoke because they started shelling and a shell landed at the base of this tree. I went outside and my great coat was like a lace curtain and everything in my haversack was smashed. I had the Jewish soldiers' prayer book; it was a thin volume, with special things in. There was a shrapnel hole right the way through it and I still have it today. You can poke you finger straight through the prayer book, it is a good souvenir I suppose.

I saw the war out in Italy. One time just at the end of the war, my unit went into Austria. The fighting was over, the Mongols were just surrendering, and they had been fighting with the Germans.

My unit was in charge of the camp for a short while. I was booking the names and all the details of all these refugees and camp victims who were coming in. Men in one half women in the other. Quite a harrowing experience really, it didn't mean a lot to us, as we had been too busy to realise what was going on.

In my army travels I have been to many countries. Starting with Ireland, then over to Africa, from Africa to Italy, from Italy to Greece when the communists started, then back to Italy, then back to Egypt for a rest. I then travelled from Egypt in convoy through the Sinai, into Palestine, from there to Syria and then back again to Italy. So I had a good 'Cooks Tour.'

While I was with the Counter Mortar section, one day I woke up and I thought, "I have been here three years and in action pretty well all the time." I just had a feeling, I don't know why, that it can't go on, something's got to happen. That day the Counter Mortar section was waiting by our jeeps watching the Durham Light Infantry attacking the San Marino Mountain. Very, very steep mountains all around and they were bringing them down by the stretcher load. Then the Germans started sending mortar bombs over and one blew the front off the jeep that I was standing by. I got wounded in the leg, my friend lost his leg, another chap had a piece in his bottom and someone else had a hole in his chest and died. So I consider that I was very lucky. But I knew that it was going to happen: it was most peculiar really.

I was also 'mentioned in Despatches'. There were three from my unit that were mentioned, don't ask me what it was for I don't really know. I think they said it was 'devotion to duty' and we received the Oakleaf.

I didn't have many problems in being Jewish. In the first unit I was in, the Territorial unit, I did have a bit of anti-Semitism from the CO himself, plus some of the officers. As I said I wasn't very happy with that unit anyway. It wasn't name calling, just underhanded things. Like one day they ran a big dance for the officers, and I was put in charge of the bar. After the dance they told me that a bottle of whisky had gone missing; now I hadn't had it, no way, but they insisted that I had had it. Just a lot of sniping, because they were a horrible lot anyway.

I was unaware what was going on with the Jews, as I was too busy fight-

81

ing. I didn't know what was going on at all. We didn't get the radio or newspapers.

I remember wandering into a vineyard in Italy. There were beautiful bunches of grapes hanging down, and I just picked a bunch of grapes. I don't know what it was, whether there was a German machine gun watching, or whether it was wired up, I don't know. But as I picked the grapes, there was this firing sound, so I ran off!

Another time I was wandering round, seeing what I could find and I found a German bunker built of rocks with planks on the top and I looked through a hole. There inside, were four Germans, all sitting at the table, not a mark on them, they were all dead. Just sitting there, dead. It must have been concussion I suppose, because we had been shelling all night and day. I didn't go in, as the place could have been booby-trapped; I had to be very careful.

I did find one booby trap in a cottage in Africa. We went in and there was a bottle of wine on the table and the fellow I was with went to get this bottle of wine and I said, "Leave it alone."

I could see a detonator in the neck of the bottle; it would have gone off if he'd picked it up. Outside there was a burned out German tank, with horrible burned bodies in the tank and there was one head on its own on the ground. You get cynical you see, and I said, " Oh it's only a German." and I kicked it like a football and it went rolling down the hill. You thought nothing of it; you got hardened to it.

I was with the Counter Mortar unit, with this young Lieutenant, who was driving the jeep. We came to this bridge which had been blown up. There was this great big hole in the middle, where the bomb had gone through and the Germans were still shelling the bridge. So we had to wait in-between shells and then take a chance and go across which we did. We shot forward and we went straight down over this big hole and onto the other side and we were O.K.

We found this big house, and we heard voices, and two of us we crept in. We heard the voices coming from the cellar so we crept down and opened the door and saw all these British soldiers sitting there. We said we wanted some water and they told us that there was a well outside in the yard. One of them shouted, "I wouldn't go there if I was you!"
However, we went to this well and it must have been covered by a

German machine gun, which started to fire so we didn't get our water.

Arnold was part of the allied invasion of Italy, the supposed soft under-belly of occupied Europe. In September 1943 the US Seventh and British Eight Armies, Led by General Patton and General Montgomery landed at Salerno, south of Naples.

In January 1944 an amphibious landing took place at Anzio but it took another six months before Rome fell in June.

Rookery House is a Grade 2 Listed Georgian building that nestles behind the ornate Italian gardens in Rookery Park. In 1991 the Friends of Rookery House were founded to make local people aware of the historic value of the house and the role it could play in educational and community use.

As part of that use the Friends of the Rookery became involved in 1940's Living History project, entitled, "Dig for Victory." The clocks in the house were turned back and local school children arrived as evacuees under the watchful eye of Mrs Spooner, the mistress of the house. The children learnt "Make do and Mend"; cooked carrot cakes and stew with the house's cook, affectionately known as Aunty Doris. They also dug up Lady Spooner's gardens for vegetables and even experienced an air raid!

At the end of the day the children would gather in the house's ballroom and listen to the Friends tell real life stories of the war. Although the house wasn't commandeered for military use the park did have ack-ack guns and barrage balloons. German Aircraft would navigate their way along the canals in an attempt to bomb factories such as Dunlops. The guns and balloons in the park were part of the defence system to prevent the Luftwaffe being successful.

Our first reminiscence comes from Mrs Osborn, who as a British citizen experienced the rarity of Nazi occupation.

Mrs Osborn.

I lived on the Channel Islands during the Second World War. We were occupied by the German forces, and I must say they treated us very well, which we didn't expect. It was rather a hard time, in as much as food got shorter and shorter and so did everything else. By the end of the five years we were so short of food we'd eat cats and dogs and some of the horses went but not necessarily to the local people. The Germans had brought in a lot of foreign workers and they really were hungry, whereas the local people could manage.

We went scrumping, but we used to do more than that. If there was anything that the Germans left lying about we would nick it, but we didn't feel you were nicking, you were helping the war effort.

One Friday in June 1940 the Germans flew over the island and they bombed the harbour. In those days we exported a lot of tomatoes and the lorries were already loaded. The Germans thought it was ammunition, which it wasn't, it was tomatoes. So we had tomato sauce forever!

We were badly bombed, so we shut up shop and most of us moved out of town, if we could. So the next day all was fine, until they flew over again about midday and the town emptied. Sunday afternoon they occupied. Just like that, they flew in. And Monday when we went into work there were Germans everywhere.

Evacuation was available for all the British men of military age and boats were laid on for them and expectant mothers and children, but it was optional. That happened a week, ten days before we were occupied. In that time everything was so quiet. We could have gone, but we delayed too long. We were bombed on the Friday and had there been boats between Friday and Sunday the island would have emptied.

The Germans took all our radios, not in the early days about twelve months after. If you were found with a radio set, you were imprisoned. Sometimes on the island and until France was invaded, islanders were sent to France and that was pretty awful. Very often it was the men and they had to leave their wives and children.

My father had a radio hidden under an ashtray, which sat in the middle of the table. So whoever came didn't realise what it was. If Churchill was speaking we were all there listening. We used to share the earphones and have one each.

There were some printers who had put out a newssheet, that was printed privately and then sent round but one was caught and went to Germany for a spell, but he came back. Some came back like him but others died when they were in Germany.

The first German I met came into the teashop where I worked. He came in and went up for coffee and we didn't know whether to charge him or not. And the manageress said, "I'm not giving him coffee for free, charge him!" When he came down he gave me German Marks, and I didn't know the valuation so he said, "Keep it."

Another time, a German came in and left his bicycle outside. The Manageress soon closed the shop. I was so annoyed that I had to wait for him to finish that I brought his bike inside and I thought, 'Silly fool.' so I punctured his tyres and then I left. I can hear to this day the air easing out of the tyres! I went upstairs and I said to the waitress, "We will take his money and let him out when he is ready to go." I heard no more.

It was very much like kids having a swipe at the grownups. I mean the grownups were doing the same, if you could knock a German you did. I don't mean physically but in other ways. For example, they had stacks of logs where they had cut our trees down and if a German wasn't looking you'd nick one. You didn't think of it as stealing it was fun, it was giving them one in the eye. I never got into trouble, I think that I was too young. My father did a lot of silly things and he was never caught.

The first Germans who came were very classy men and we were very short of men in general, because they had gone to join the forces. There were a lot of German babies born on the island but the Germans weren't allowed to marry the women from the island. After the war, in Jersey they tarred and feathered these girls, but in Guernsey they turned a blind eye as a lot of them left the island.

However, I think three Germans that I know of came back after the war and married local girls.

They obviously had slept with them, but no more than that. I suppose the equivalent would be the girls in England going out with the Yanks during the war but it wasn't popular. I think if you're male and female you are bound to get together. I was too young. If Guernsey girls went out with the Germans, it was because they wanted to, they didn't force them. In fact there was a house where they had brought girls from France to serve the Germans. The girls went because they wanted to go. In one or two cases where Germans did wrong they were punished.

We had a lot of amateur shows and we weren't allowed to sing the National Anthem, so we used to finish with Land of Hope and Glory. The

Salvation Army was disbanded because they wore uniform. But we were treated well. If the Germans wanted anything in a shop, it wasn't commandeered, they bought it. Fair enough they paid with Marks, which we all thought was no good, but they paid for the goods with them.

To some extent we knew what was going on in the rest of the war. Some had the radio and if you didn't have one news filtered through.

About two and a half years after the occupation, they decided to take the English to Germany. These included children and people up to the age of seventy.

When the notice came for 'English born and their dependants' to leave we weren't given a reason and at the time we thought maybe it was repatriation. We just didn't know and we could take only what we could carry. That would have been September 1942 and I would have been just nineteen.

We were in prison camps but they were nothing like the horror stories you hear. However, the first one was in North Germany, which was dreadful. Then we went to Southern Germany, which was really quite comfortable. We were put in barracks, behind barbed wire with guards, like you see on the films. We were hungry but by then we weren't frightened of the Germans any more.

The French liberated us and then we made our way towards home. Once we were liberated by the French the gates were thrown open. We were in the middle of the French and the Americans coming through Germany. Once the Americans knew that there was an English camp, the women used to come with cakes and bread, you wouldn't believe it.

I was in a prison camp for two and a half years. I think it was more horrible for the older people. There were some things that were hard to get used to and our way of life was different to what it is now.

Men and women were separated, but you could mix during the day and I suppose in each barracks there was at least seventy people. In my particular barracks there was five years olds to twenty-year-olds. You all bathed together, there was a shower room, and we all had three minutes to undress, shower and get dressed. I can understand mothers not wanting to bath with their daughters and some were rather funnily shaped and we were all so shy in those days but for someone my age it was a giggle.

We couldn't get out of the camp so in the day we would do our own washing, the cooking was done, we had Red Cross parcels, we knitted a lot and sewed a lot. One of the wooden huts was turned into a concert hall. I am not artistic in any way but I was a general dog's body to someone who was. I was told to put the paint here and to move that there. So I was occupied. There where teachers in the camp. You could learn any language but Russian as there wasn't anyone there who could speak it. You could learn short hand typing. Really there was quite a lot to do. Jersey and Guernsey even had their own football and netball teams.

Our Red Cross parcels came in wooden boxes and there was a toy for every child in the camp. I painted them. The YMCA supplied all this. The Red Cross supplied the food, but the YMCA supplied all our other needs. There was a magnificent library and if you were into poetry reading you could request a book but it might take six months to arrive.

One of the guards we had was a prisoner of war in the 1914/18 war in England and he was very nice to us. He had a dog, which he used to walk round the camp with and we used to feed it.

We knew that we were going to be liberated by the Yanks or the French. One day we were on a hill and we could actually see the French coming down one side.

In the camp we had sewing machines and we made a big Red Cross flag. As soon as we were liberated we flew our flag. The Germans soon left.

I didn't feel like I was imprisoned, life went on just the same and we weren't ill-treated. Because of the Red Cross we were well fed and when I got to England I was ten stone ten, my sister, who was in England was seven stone something and she lived in Leeds. When I came back from Germany, I was as fat as a house and as brown as a berry, and my sister was as skinny as a rake and white, white, white. They hadn't had any sun. People used to look at my sister and would say that they thought it was her who was in the prisoner of war camp. I mean I looked so healthy and I was really.

We were all glad to get home back to Guernsey. Once we were home there were all the liberation forces and that was how I met my husband. There were about two fellows to every girl, so you had a choice, which was fun!

I think, to think that all Germans are bad is wrong, because they're not, it was just the odd one. The ones in power perhaps. I don't think that we should forget the war but I think that we should forget the bitterness that went with the war.

Sutton Coldfield is now a thriving suburb. However, when Mrs Hartland lived in Walmley it was still a village. She lived on a farm, which lay at the back of the village church, St John's. There is a war memorial at the village cross roads dedicated to all those that gave their lives during the two world wars.

Mrs Hartland.

I was a member of a family of three and my father was a farmer and because he was a farmer he didn't have to go to war. We had buildings all the way round the farmhouse, which contained animals, so as soon as the air-raid sirens went my father had to go out and take his gun with him. So that if anything happened, if a bomb set fire to a building or an animal was hurt in any way he was there and was able to put the animal out of its pain and shoot it.

I was collected most mornings by an older child. There were no street-lights, no road signs or street numbers. We very quickly made our way to school taking with us our small boxes, which contained a biscuit and chocolate or some cocoa with some sugar and some sultanas and also our gas masks and our identity cards. We got into school, which was dark with shutters over the windows. When the air raids took place we had to march quickly into the playground and down into the shelters which ran underneath the playground. We took with us our gas masks and our boxes containing our food and we went down quite happily. It was possible that we would remain there for about half an hour or maybe an hour, we were never sure. This was our village school and at that time it was for both Junior and Seniors. So obviously the older children used to look after us.

The shelters were in the playground and the only thing visible was a lid, which looked like planks that were over a hole. The planks were removed, which took you down a concrete stairway to a concrete tunnel with wooden seats on either side and the tunnel went right across the playground, from one end to the other.

If we were fortunate to get through the day, we went home at night and we walked up Fox Hollies Road and if you heard a siren go off, you always knocked on the first door you came to and they always took you in. You didn't know who they were and if no one came to the door quickly you went in anyway, because doors were never locked in those days.

It was very frightening and you didn't know whether you would get home to your mum and dad because situated in Walmley you were between Erdington that made ammunitions and the aerodrome with Spitfires in Castle Bromwich. There was also the power station and if the bombs dropped on that it would cut out everybody's power. You were always very kind to everyone and they all spoke to each other. And you were always helpful to anybody you met in the street.

Obviously all our food was rationed. If you were in a position to hear that there were bananas or oranges at the local shop, which was about half a mile away, all the children were sent there by their parents to go and queue. You had to stand for two or three hours just to get one banana or one orange and that would have to last you for some time. Also a quarter of sweets would have to last a month.

I remember very well the night that Coventry was bombed. At that stage we had an Anderson Shelter in the garden and it was a corrugated shelter. This particular night, the siren went about half past six in the evening and the planes started to drum across and we could hear them directly above us. They continued to fly over through the night, they were turning round and coming back over, so we got traffic both ways. My father came to the door of the shelter and he said, " My word Dorothy, Coventry has been bombed tonight."

That night you could see a red sky right across the sky from the fire that had left Coventry almost devastated. It was at least twenty miles away.

The Germans were very keen to bomb the power station, as it would put a lot of places out of action. One particular night they dropped bombs on the power station. The wind was in the wrong direction and the bombs blew north and we had a bomb in two of our fields and a neighbouring house had one in their garden. It created a huge crater and for many years after the war it was still a crater and that was where we would get our frogs' spawn. We were very fortunate that night.

There was an American service camp but I was too young to appreciate the American soldiers. Quite a lot of girls got involved with the American soldiers; some of the girls were very fortunate as they got silk stockings.

Penns Lane had a large American air base.

We had prisoners of war working on the land. We had two lots, German and Italian. I did write to one of the Germans after the war. He was called Alfons, who was only about eighteen at the time

My mother used to cook very well and we were very fortunate having a good garden and were able to grow our own vegetables. We would always have a good meal at lunchtime and mother always gave us fruit or made an apple pie.

I was always sent down to the cow shed, where the prisoners of war that we had were and I would take them perhaps a piece of apple pie and custard or something like that. They were brought in the morning and collected at night and they worked on the land. Both the prisoners we had were German. Alfons was a very young chap and I did hear from him after the war. He got married and had a family.

They had their pudding or cake every day that my mum sent them. They were too young to be hostile. They used to do any job on the farm and then they would go back to the prison camp.

We also had British prisoners of war. One was called Mr Maddox, who still lives in Walmley today and one called Mr Carter and they both came home from the prisoner of war camp. When they came home Mr Carter weighed approximately four stone. Being on a farm and having chickens we were very fortunate and had more food than a lot people and I remember my mother finding a little bit extra to help these men put some weight on, and to get back to their good heath, which they did. Mr Carter only died about five years ago and Mr Maddox lives very locally to us, in Walmley.

He had two small children at the time and he was actually recorded missing and Mrs Maddox was very upset as she thought that she wouldn't see her husband again. Then there was a telegram from the War Office. The farm and her house are more or less half a mile away and the postman ran more or less the whole length of Fox Hollies Road to take this telegram. It said that Mr Maddox had been found and was on his way home. He did manage to come home. He stepped down from the train at the local station. He was in a very poor state of repair, but he lived and he is still alive today.

The most thing that sticks out in my memory is how kind and how trusting everybody was to us. Because you didn't really know which day was going to be your last day. So you were always very kind and helpful and you did the best you could for everybody.

Ann Legge is an Edwardian. King Edward VII was on the throne when she was born so when she was a little girl the Great War raged throughout Europe and Africa. Her husband was in the Royal Navy during that war and experienced the horrors of Gallipoli.

Mrs Legge.

I come from Surrey, from Dorking, which is near Guildford. That is where I was during the First World War. I went to school there. I don't remember that much about the First World War except that it was always dark at nighttime. But I don't remember anything vividly at all. I was young and I was very Victorian at that time. All I remember was that it was always dark and I remember listening to the soldiers in the street.

In the last war I was married with a family of my own. I lived in Erdington and I still have the air raid shelter where I used to put my children to bed. I still have it in my garden. When we first started having air raids I would put my children to bed in their own bed and then when the air raids increased I would put them to bed in the shelter. My husband wouldn't stay in the air raid shelter, he said, "If I'm going to be killed I and going to lie in my bed and enjoy it.' I used to spend the evenings running back wards and forwards to see if he was still alive, because the raid got very heavy locally.

And then eventually we were evacuated. We went out to Exford, which is in Derbyshire. It's a village and there was a woman there called Mrs Barsey Clarke and her husband was Major Barsey Clarke. When she saw these children arrive in the village she wasn't quite sure what to do.

I had this scruffy-curly haired bunch of children. I was with them, as a message came through that they wanted a strong woman who was a mother, to come out and run this cottage for these children. So I was sent out, I took my baby who was two and my other two children were all ready there.

We were sent to the cottage and I did all the cooking, the washing, the ironing and dealing with head lice. There were no modern facilities, there was an old range in the kitchen that boiled the water, but there were no modern facilities at all. It was very rough really and there were no carpets or anything and Mrs Barsey Clarke used to knit these huge mats for the children to sleep on. We were quite a happy community really and I got ever so fond of the children. They were lovely in spite of their head lice and scabies. I had never come across head lice before, so it was quite a shock when the nurse came round one morning and said, "Oh Mrs Legge I have just been to see your children in school. Do you know that they have dirty heads?" I said, "No they can't have I washed all their heads last night." They had beautiful shiny hair and I had no idea what head lice looked like. It was awful; night after night I had to deal with it. I put stuff on their heads and tied their heads up and left them over night.

My life was turned upside down and my husband was still at home and I had so much to deal with. I do remember the raid on Coventry because I could see it from our village. It was very vivid; it was like a fire works display.

I had a hip bath, which I used to bring in and put by this old grate in the evening and fill it with hot water from the range, and bath all these children every night. They used to go to bed looking really shiny and lovely. We would have bed time stories. It was a lovely family.

One night I was having a bath myself and there was a raid, and of course we never locked the door and the air raid warden came in and I shouted, "You can't come in I'm having a bath." It was in the country but we would get odd bombs dropped.

I have always worked with children and these children had different life styles. I remember one morning, little Thelma came up to me and said, "Miss can I have a bit of paper? Our Rosie wants a bit of paper."

"Oh is she going to draw me a picture?" I replied.

"No she wants to wipe her bum!" Thelma stated.

Sometimes the parents would come up for the weekend, which was nice for the children. I had about sixteen children in the end including three of my own.

The day the war broke out I was taking our children to school, and war was declared that very morning. As I came home there were three youths,

(I have never forgotten this), they were about seventeen, waiting for their call up. They were laughing and were full of excitement. Little did they know what was in store for them! I knew, and I felt very sad. They were so jubilant that they were going to come out of the factories and going to France. Of course people didn't go abroad then for their holidays did they?

The day the war ended, my husband was home then. We pulled up trees and walked all night, we carried our babies round the streets. My husband went down Spring Lane to pull up trees. It was very dramatic, it was wonderful.

Just to think we had night after night in the shelter, then we were spilt up and my husband was away for a long time.

During the First World War he became a communist. He turned communist because of the way that Churchill ran the war. He thought he was using all these young lads of seventeen as targets. In the First World War, when he was at the Dardanelles he had actually seen young fellows running across territory to draw the enemy out and the young lads were shot down.

My husband was broken hearted when he saw this. One particular night he slept on the beach and every one else slept on the hills because the fighting was so thick. So he dug a hole in the sand with his hand and he had a jolly good night's sleep.

The next morning he went up the hill and everybody was fast asleep. They all thought he was killed.

He was an Air Raid Warden in the Second World War. He died in 1961. He was a wonderful man, and although he was a communist he was fond of his fellow workers. He was always looking after people and trying to put the world right. He was an idealist, a good man, very caring and he used to get very upset when his fellow workers were taken down. You would have liked Harry and he never stopped talking. He was older than me; I didn't like younger men, as they were too irresponsible. I had only known him three months before we were married. I would have changed my mind if I had waited any longer! I met him on a poultry farm. He had an old hen and he came down to look for a cockerel and he found me instead! We had four children and I have six grandsons.

The Air Raid Wardens would meet at the school. They used to have meetings and fire watch and he would be out all night fire watching.

The war was a great upheaval in our lives; there was always so much going on. I was so glad when it was over as it was horrible.

Doris Acton is probably better known as Aunty Doris and loved for her wonderful and famous Carrot cake and Bread Pudding, which people queued for at Rookery House!

As part of the House's Living History day Doris would mesmerise the children with her stories about being an evacuee especially when she told them she lived in a sweet shop. Sadly, that particular experience wasn't as wonderful as it could have been!

Doris Acton.

I was an evacuee from Erdington and a very dilapidated bus took us into the countryside to a village hall. Then the women and some of the men, who lived in the village, came and picked out the child they wanted.

They looked at us to see if we had nits, to see if we had washed behind our ears, and asked if we wet ourselves or wet the bed. They chose the one they thought would do the most work for them. The woman, who picked me, had a sweet shop and had four children, all younger than me. At the time I was evacuated I was just nine.

She had these four very little children, two of whom were still in nappies, one a very young baby. I had to clean the babies up and change their nappies or towelling, as it was then, and wash them. That was terrible.

Since it was a sweet shop her children always wanted sweets, sweets and more sweets. So she used to give them my sweet ration as well as their own so I didn't have any sweets all the time I was there.

All the local children went to the village school, but the children who had been evacuated there went one week in the morning and the next week in the afternoon. So the village children went at other times. We didn't mix. It wasn't until we were about twelve, doing our eleven plus exams that the evacuees and the children of the village all sat in the same room. I had passed by then and eventually I came back and went to what was then Erdington Girls Grammar School. Oh I was a clever child!

It was a relief to me as although there was bombing and such going on, I'd rather be back at home, than looking after all those children and being their servant.

I didn't enjoy being an evacuee and my brother was sent to a different village, which made it worse.

My mother and father stayed in Birmingham on Kingsbury Road. Father was the Head Air Raid Warden for that district and when we came back, he was working for a brewery, so he could get large wooden barrels. He put these at the bottom of the garden and, when there was an air raid on, we would jump in a barrel, sit on a little stool and pull a lid over the top.

When father was on duty one night, a bomb dropped down the road. So he went down there and it had only made a small hole, so he thought that it hadn't exploded. He said that on the way to work in the morning, when it was light, he would come back to see if it was a bomb or just shrapnel or something that had landed. Well, the next morning he forgot to go and was on his way to work when he heard such a bang go off. It was an unexploded bomb after all, and if he hadn't forgotten he would have been standing on the edge of the crater when it went off. It was only a small one but it blew the back of one house off. No one was hurt, fortunately.

When the school holidays were on I used to go to my grandmother's in Newborough; it wasn't very far away. I was at grandmothers when a gypsum* mine blew up. It was where they used to store bombs, detonators and other things ready for going off to war. Stupidly, the war office put prisoners-of-war to help down there, and you can guess what they did. They sabotaged it. The site now is a war memorial.

Fifteen of my relations, who lived near by and worked in another mine next to this one, were killed. There were farms above the mine, so farmers were killed too, and one or two cottages were blown up as well. They never found the people on the farm and all the houses were just reduced to rubble.

* Gypsum mine. Gypsum is used in the making of plaster of paris.

Cairo in the 1940's conjures up memorable and magical images such as those in the Bogart movie, Casablanca. After the fall of France, North Africa became the only theatre of war where both armies could meet on the stage of the Western Desert. General Erwin Rommel fought and lost

to the British at El Alamein, who were led by the famous General Montgomery. I came across Joe and Marjorie Ovadia from Sutton Coldfield, who experienced the war years in Cairo. A story of Nightclubs, romance and spies feature in their reminiscences!

Joe and Marjorie Ovadia.

The year is 1936 and I have finished my French education at a French college in Cairo. The time came to get a job and I was employed at the Cairo Stock Exchange.

For three years before World War Two business was booming and the job was very interesting.

Then 1939 came and with the war things were very difficult at the stock exchange, in view of the fact that people were looking ahead to the war and not looking at buying or selling shares.

At that time I was playing in a band as an amateur at various functions, weddings banquets etc. The stock exchange work was coming in very slow and was also very little that I decided to leave the job and become a professional musician.

A band was formed and engagements were coming in pretty fast. In view of the fact that a great number of musicians were Italian and Italy was at war with Britain, the British authorities interned them. However this went on for a while until one night, when playing in a nightclub, a number of service people, including British ATS, came to spend their evening. After a while an ATS sergeant came up me and asked if a member of her party could sing a song with the band. This was accepted and eventually a very shy person in a British uniform came onto the stage and decided to sing, 'Yours'.

Well, she was a great success, people kept on applauding, which kept her on the stage for a little longer than anticipated.

This gave me the opportunity for me in between the applause to ask this young shy ATS for her telephone number. Surprising as it seems, she gave me her telephone number as GHQ, which meant General Headquarters 323. At first I thought that it was a joke, but the next day I decided to ring her up and was very surprised, not only to talk to this young ATS, but also for her to accept an invitation to lunch. Her name was Marjorie Craig, Royal signal corps, based at GHQ Cairo.

The conversation during lunch was very interesting; it appeared that Marjorie was one of the very few girls sent from Cheltenham war office to Cairo, to relieve the men who went to the desert. Apparently Marjorie and her friends sailed from Scotland in a twenty one thousand ton ship and for eight weeks she was at sea, calling at South Africa and then eventually to Egypt. War was on and quite a lot of incidents took place at sea. They were quite happy and relieved when they reached Port Tewfick in Egypt, before being transferred to Cairo.

Her job was a difficult one, working on Tele-printers under ground, with very few staff members, as the men were all in the western desert. The girls had to work a twenty four-hour shift.

Despite a lot of trouble and unsettled times due to certain members of the local population where WD vehicles were overturned, she managed to remain in her uniform as civilian clothes were not allowed at the time.

Marjorie and I kept going out together although it was difficult for me, as I was busy in the evening playing with the band. Very often Marjorie came and sat in the same establishment where the band was playing. However, I had to play in various establishments, first class hotels and during a few nights at the Mena House Hotel, near the Pyramids. I had the opportunity to see Mr Churchill, President Roosevelt, and Chiang Kai-Chek, who were believed to be staying at that hotel during a conference.

Another interesting point was when I was playing at Shepherds Hotel, which was only for civilians and officers. It was noticed that a British Major, or a person believed to be a British Major was coming to the bar for several nights. The same British Major was seen also at the bar a few days later dressed as an Egyptian Lord! People talk and very often officers would talk to the band and me about various things. It was interesting to know that apparently this so called British major and Egyptian Lord was a German spy, and was arrested on his house boat on the Nile, soon after, about three or four o'clock in the morning!

Time passed and 1945 came and we were nearing the end of the war. It was time for Marjorie and her unit to return to England. Naturally we were engaged, but papers for the wedding were not received, as there was a lot of paper work and red tape to go through so many army rules and regulations.

However, twenty four hours prior to Marjorie's embarkation, I managed through the British embassy in Cairo, to secure the necessary papers which were passed to Marjorie's Commanding Officer and permission to marry was granted. This took place in June 1945 in Cairo.

I continued to play in the band and I was made in charge of the NAAFI bands for officers' clubs. After the wedding, the band and I moved to the officers' club in Ismalia, naturally with Majorie, and we remained in the Canal Zone until 1949 when Marjorie and I decided to sail for England. This took place in August 1949, reaching Tilbury docks and then proceeding to Lincolnshire, which was Marjorie's home base.

Having taken a job with P&O company in their office in 1950, Marjorie, two daughters and myself remained in Lincolnshire until 1960 when my employers transferred me to their Birmingham office.

In 1998 Marjorie joined the W.R.A.C. Association where, "Surprise, surprise" she met an ex A.T.S. by the name of Gwen Finney who she last saw in 1942 in Cheltenham where they both served. In fact she was Marjorie's Section Corporal. They have now become firm friends.

Another amazing thing happened early in the year 2000. Marjorie read an article in, 'YOURS' magazine from a man who was trying to contact members of the Cairo Amateur Dramatic and Musical Society who performed in Cairo in 1942/43. Marjorie was one of those ladies and this gentleman only lives 10 miles away. So she contacted him and he still has in his possession programmes autographed by Marjorie and they both appear on photos together.

Marjorie and I meet this gentleman on a regular basis and all three of us are now in our eighties.

It's never too late to meet again!

Joe and Marjorie outside pyramids in Egypt.

Mountie R Freeman is third on the left, back row. Marjorie is fourth on the left front row. Marjorie recently met up with Mr Freeman after all these years.

Joe and Marjorie Ovadia, taken in North Africa.

As mentioned in the introduction the thought of, "Father once fighting Father" came to mind when I saw those young Germans in Calais. The waste and human tragedy in any war is immense and if war is ever to be averted, if peace is ever to be established, the thoughts, the feelings, the memories of both sides have to be heard. I thought it was important that someone who experienced the war from another perspective should be given the chance to give his or her story.

I was fortunate to meet Frank Feld who originally came from Germany but has lived the majority of his life in England with his English wife, children and grand children.

Frank Feld resident of Sutton Coldfield.

I was called up in 1941 on my seventeenth birthday, October the 3rd. In Osijek Yugoslavia, I was serving there.

I was brought to the barracks in Pancevo. But I don't think they knew what to do with me and it was about a fortnight before I was transferred to a place called Welika Kikinda. This was a week before Christmas 1941. From there we went to Poland to Crackow and we had some more training there, with the Seventh Alpine Corps.

From there we went to Zitomir in the Ukraine, and they were starting a battle that summer of 42. It was bad enough just going there but it wasn't too bad because it was summer time. But in the winter when we got to Stalingrad, that was a very bad one, 1942. Because we were there about nine or ten months in Stalingrad in the worst winter.

We were trying to get into the city, but they, (the Russians) wouldn't let us get in. We thought it was all in one place but Stalingrad is on the estuary. We got to the outskirts of the town, we were that close.

We had no winter clothes when we were there, only summer clothes and what you could find you would put round you, even in the trenches. We were living in the trenches because there were no tents. Some did freeze to death. I was one of the lucky ones. I was one of the lucky ones to get back.

I saw the Russian soldiers every day and I fought them every day. Even in the winter they would come, but you could never see in front of you because of the snowstorms, but they still did come. It was so cold about 44 or 45 degrees below zero. I don't know why you had to stand and guard in that weather but you did and then when you had to change guards, he might be frozen to the ground – dead and you couldn't use the cannons because the oil froze.

I was wounded in the head; I still have my wound there. They shot me, you know. So that's how I got back to Germany for recuperation. I went to recuperate in the Hartz Mountains in Germany. I was in solitary confinement for a while and I was then put into a penal company.

I was going on guard duty and the relief guard did not arrive on time so the company sergeant made us load our guns. We went out onto the parade ground. It was raining and the company sergeant wanted to have an inspection of the guns to see if they were clean. Well, we all put a bit of rag on the bayonets so the rain didn't get on them. The sergeant found something wrong with mine and he went on and on. He called me a gypsy so I bashed him with my loaded gun around the face. If it wasn't loaded it wouldn't have been so bad but as it was loaded it was a very grievous offence. It is a serious offence to hit a superior officer anyway but with a loaded gun this was worse. I was not 21 years of age and I was court-martialled for 12 months solitary but it was reduced to six months.

I served my sentence in Germany. I never saw daylight for six months. There were a couple of bricks that were out of place so I could tell it was either day or night. There was many a British soldier that did six years in prison and they didn't need counselling. I was in that cell in Halle. There was no floor, only a grid where running water flowed underneath. In the corner there was a wash basin but the tap didn't work. But you could hear the drip, drip of the tap. No matter what you did you could not stop the thing! There wasn't a bench or anything. You were allowed to take your bed down at 8.00 at night and you put it back in the wall at six o'clock in the morning. For toilets you had a bucket and food came through the flap. There were no newspapers, nothing, nothing at all.

For the first fortnight I used to walk up and down the cell until I was exhausted then sit on the grid and listen to the water. After that I used to just stare at the walls.

After the six months they sent me to Cherbourg in France to the penal company. You had no rank, you were a prisoner and we were there to fight, we were waiting for the invasion. We were 10, 11 miles outside Cherbourg. We did a lot of marching and we were guarded, as you weren't free to do what you liked. We were prisoners.

The invasion came and we were over run. I remember the night the gliders came and the sky was all lit up like a lovely display. It was phosphorous to light up the landing paths. I was in a cornfield and I had some brandy. I listened to some voices nearby and as I didn't understand the language then I knew they weren't ours. I thought, "This is it." I thought when I was sent to the penal company that I wouldn't get back at all so now it didn't matter that much.

After the invasion we went to Holland, crossed the Rhine at Aachen and then we reached the river Elbe where the Russians and Americans were. We asked in the village if they had seen any British and they said that they had come through the village only four hours ago. They weren't far way. So that night a fisherman rowed us across the Elbe but he didn't want to go to where we wanted. However, I then managed to get home.

I was arrested in December 1945 seven months after the war had ended.

They came for me at five o'clock in the morning, as I had no discharge papers. I was then taken to prison in Germany and then to Belgium. I then was transferred to Moreton in Marsh in England. I was also in Penns Lane in Sutton Coldfield.

I met my wife, who is a Brummie, when I was in Stratford upon Avon. I had some good times and bad times.

When looking at photographs of the war one can not help but be moved by images of children at railway stations waiting to be evacuated to the countryside. The children wear identity labels, carry gas masks and of course there is always a Teddy Bear somewhere to give comfort! During the early part of the war nearly one and a half million children were evacuated from the cities and sent to the countryside for safety. Dorothy Fleming, like Aunty Doris tells her story as an evacuee.

Dorothy Fleming.

Yes it was my parent's decision to send me away as an evacuee; (my father was in the Army at that time). We did not know where we were going.

Our parents were circulated by letter, via the school – Burbury Street Junior and Senior School, advising them to allow their children to be moved, ' To a place of safety.'

No notices were displayed like this. The only notices I can remember from that period are such as 'CARELESS TALK COSTS LIVES', 'DIG FOR VICTORY', 'WOMEN – THE LAND ARMY NEEDS YOU.'

I was 12 years old in 1939 and together with my brother and my mother, (who was a voluntary helper); we were marched to Hockley Station in Birmingham. We all had a ticket placed on us bearing our name and name of school.

We journeyed to Evesham where we were taken to the village hall for the night. My recollections of this night were being given a blanket, mug of cocoa and something to eat, and sleeping on a hard floor!

My brother and I were fortunate enough to have our mother with us, but some of the children were in tears, feeling very homesick and calling for their mothers.

The next morning we were literally chosen by our prospective foster parents. Naturally the pretty girls were chosen first. Now as a parent and grandparent, I can understand the hesitation of foster parents at that time, some of the children were very poor, and possible their language and behaviour left much to be desired. But, I must stress there was no vandalism in those days, just high spirits.

We were not advised what clothes to take. Gas masks and ration book were top priority of the day. There must have been a Billeting Officer in charge but I was too young to be aware of this.

Accommodation was varied but adequate. Food rationing was in operation by then and we only had a very basic diet. Oranges and bananas were never seen!

I was unhappy at my first billet, so I was moved to my second billet in the village. This was because the lady at the first billet had taken in three girls and found she couldn't cope.

I do remember that these foster parents were being paid by the government to billet us. My second billet I can only describe as awful. My most vivid memory is of feeling unwanted and also being served lunch one day, which consisted of rabbit, which had not been cleaned at all. I still shudder at that memory.

My third billet was with a charming couple and their daughter at Thatcholm in Harvington. I stayed in a beautiful thatched cottage; their daughter Margaret and I shared a low-beamed bedroom. I corresponded with my foster parents, Mr and Mrs Collett for many years, and I believe their daughter now lives in Eckington.

Our education was not in school with the other children but took place in the village hall, supervised by our 'own' teacher – Miss Bryan – whom I can remember to this day, she was a lovely lady. I personally lost out in maths and sciences, but discovered lots about nature and the countryside. One day we had a nature lesson and found "The Lenches"* and on another occasion we learned about different cloud formations and the weather.

We were children from a built-up area of Birmingham, who had already suffered both stress from bombing and also sleepless nights. Then, to be moved from one's home environment was very traumatic. I suppose I must have been run down, when I suddenly developed abscesses and was admitted to Evesham Hospital. I remember a great fuss was made of me at the time. I was too old for the children's ward, so I was put into the ladies' ward, and I was thoroughly spoiled. I remained there for about a week to ten days.

Once or twice the dentist visited us at the village hall, complete with a very tatty dental chair. All the children were scared! After my first visit my mother decided to take me to a private dentist in Evesham. Following treatment I remember visiting a Milk Bar, and enjoying a hot mug of Ovaltine.

I left school in June 1941 aged fourteen. No ceremony or speech day, I was just presented with a certificate for elementary education.

With the men away at War, it was essential women helped with the war effort. Therefore at the beginning of July 1941 I joined the Lucas Organisation as a trainee and eventually became secretary to their personnel officer.

I only lived in Shipston for about a year in 1944. At that time my parents left Birmingham altogether to move to Shipston. I was not very happy there, so I returned to Birmingham and lived in digs until I married.

It was at Shipston where I saw the convoys passing through and I remember waving to soldiers of all nationalities. I now realise it was the start of the build up in 1944 to D- day and VJ –Day, bringing us victory and the end of the war.

*Lenches: A set of villages in Worcestershire.

Mrs Osborn gave an account of what life was like under German occupation. However, nearly all of Europe was under Nazi domination. I was privileged to have access to the very interesting reminiscences of French citizens who experienced life in an occupied Europe. The evacuation of Dunkirk, code named Operation Dynamo, successfully evacuated some 338, 000 troops. Unfortunately, this left the citizens of France to experience, 'Fortress Europe.'

A world of terror reigned especially as the Nazis tried to implement their racial laws. Also between 1939 and 1942 200, 000 French military personal had been killed and 400, 000 French citizens died in air raids or in concentration camps.

It was left to the Resistance to carry on the fight. Churchill hoped that they would, "Set Europe ablaze."

The first French person to give an account of life under the Nazi yoke is Renée Brégent from Brittany. Her niece, Sophie Brégent, teaches French at Moseley School in Birmingham.

Renée Brégent.

I was twelve years old when the war broke out and I was living in Brittany, near Lorient.

My father was arrested by the Gestapo and was held for several hours before he was released. They searched the house and found nothing. It was all because he was fishing too close to the harbour, so he just got a big fine.

We were bombarded almost every night with incendiary bombs. They went everywhere and seldom hit their target, but several houses got hit and burned and many people died.

In January 1943 they gave us twenty-four hours to leave the town around the harbour. The Germans built a submarine base; it was so strong and could never be destroyed. It is still used now and people come to visit it.

My parents went away for the night with my grandfather in a wheelbarrow. They moved a few days later 50 miles from home, until the end of the war.

I remember in June 1940, we buried my grandmother. And that day the planes were leaving for England. The family went to the cemetery and when we came home the sailors asked every man if they could have their civilian clothes. My family gave them their clothes and also food from the funeral.

Then somebody said that Lorient was an open target and so the military blew up all the tanks around us. It took several weeks to stop the fire, it was awful.

The explosions erupted several miles over the water so many people were burned to death.

My happiest memory is when the Americans came and my saddest memory is when the Germans killed several priests in St Anne d' Auray.

Jean Marais was a young man at the outbreak of the war. He was born only a few years after the First World War. The memory of that dreadful war was still fresh in the memories of most French people. When the Germans successfully breached the Maginot line a sense of dread spread across La Belle France.

Jean is a family friend of Valerie Baudon who is a French assistant in Birmingham. Here is his story.

Jean Marais.

My name is Jean Marais and in 1939 I was living in Vierzon. I was 16 and a half years old and a student at the National Professional School. (ENP). I experienced the events of March 1939, when the preparation of the war had already started. Some air-raid shelters were set up; I put myself at the disposal of the Passive Defence Corps, which appointed me in charge of the shelter next to my house.

In early September, Germany decreed general mobilisation after the attack of Poland. General Mobilisation started 2nd September 1939 at midnight.

Ex-servicemen from the First World War had tears in their eyes when they heard the news.

Requisitions of horses, lorries, cars began. Men hurried to the station to rejoin their postings. A civilian unit for the "Anti-para-troopers" was created. I enlisted in it. This was the first day of ration vouchers, fear of air raids and of enemy paratroopers landing.

The third of September came and war was declared on Germany.

On the seventh of September an air-raid warning took place. I was at the shelter, I was in charge of and I organised the arrival of the people who were coming in.

Also, several sorties in the forest of Vierzon took place by night in order to detect some possible para-troopers who may have landed there.

This dreadful war soon got the better of my patience, and with my parents' permission and cheating on my birth date I declared I was 18 and a half years old, and 'physically I looked liked it'.

I enlisted in the army in the 30th Gunner's regiment at Orleans. After three months of training in Orleans my regiment was posted to Hazebrouck (North of France), near the Belgian border.

On the 10th of May 1940 Germany attacked Holland and Belgium. My regiment entered Belgium and it was my baptism of fire. I was very frightened. Crushed by the enemy we beat a retreat. The Germans advanced by making a pincer movement. We just avoided being taken prisoner. After a few rear- guard fights and from retreat to retreat, a full rout took place.

It was on the seventeenth of June 1940 in a small village of Loiret that we heard Marshal Petain on the radio announcing that he had asked for an Armistice. There was joy among the soldiers and the civilians as this was, hopefully, the end of the nightmare.

The Armistice was signed on the twenty fifth of June. I was demobilised on the twenty seventh of June in Issoudun. I went back to Vierzon, where I found it in ruins and the whole place at a standstill. The demarcation line* cut Vierzon in two parts.

I asked the German Komandantur, which managed the town for an "Ausvesse" (pass) and I got it. I then smuggled mail into the unoccupied zone, which was forbidden by the 'Boches'.

In August 1940, after contact with some people, who like me did not accept the situation, I joined the Resistance. I escorted Allied prisoners clandestinely through the demarcation line and often as far as the Spanish border. I was in the Resistance group O.C.M (Civilian and Military Organisation). I gave information and sabotaged the enemy's phone lines.

I had often been in danger as were my resistance comrades. During a sabotaging operation enemy soldiers pursued us. We knew if we were caught, we would be shot on the spot. Many of my friends suffered this fate.

Passing over the demarcation line was also very dangerous.

I took up again my studies at the National School of Vierzon 'ENP', where on November 13th 1942 I was arrested by the Gestapo, taken to Paris to the 'Rue Des Sausaies', Gestapo Headquarters. I was interrogated and ill-treated and then taken away to Germany. I was forcibly sent to the re-education work camp. An 'A.E.L', camp at Moosach. I was imprisoned from the thirtieth of January 1943 to the twenty second of June 1943.

After leaving prison, I was forced to join the Komandos of Samelager 8. During my deportation in Germany I was forced to be in the 'Clearing Komandos'. This meant that after the allied air raids we were put in front of unexploded bombs as they were cleared. The bombs stood a good chance of exploding at any time. The saddest memory was the day when I was in Germany draining sand from the river Danube guarded by the SS whose emblem was a skull, who without reason shot a friend at my side. There were other atrocities committed by the concentration camp guards.

However, I escaped with the complicity of an Austrian woman working at the Arbeit Sam (German work Ministry) and the help of some French war prisoners who were at the Straff Komando. These ones already had seventeen escape attempts. At the time of my escape from Germany, I remember being frightened. I had to pass through two rows of electrified barbed wire, pass under the searchlights and the machine guns of the watchtowers, which were shooting at us. This was for me a terrible experience. If I was alone, I think I would have given up and been killed.

My thoughts towards the Germans were that they were the enemy, bloodthirsty savages. About 80% of them were supporters of Hitler. A few were good, but very few. All my thoughts were to see them vanquished. And set my country free.

*In 1940 France was divided in two. The occupied and the non-occupied zones.

Afterwards, after my escape from the concentration camp in Germany, I went back to the same service and also to the sabotaging of the enemy communication lines: Railtracks, phone - lines and radio-lines. I was a transmitter operator of 'Radio Paris', situated in Allouis, which was destroyed by an explosion. I also went back to my activities escorting people to Spain until the Liberation, which came on September 4th 1944.

When Paris was liberated I heard about the liberation only a few days later. I was in the region of Vierzon, sabotaging the communication lines, railway tracks, and locomotives. I was also cutting down the trees on the roadsides in order to delay the arrival of the SS Column from the Das Reich division which was coming up from the South of France. They were like the hordes of Attila, killing and burning everything on their way.

A small village near Vierzon, Saint Hilaire De Court, experienced the same tragedy as Auradour-Sur-Glanes *

With the liberation of Paris my feeling was that the Nazis were done for and that Germany had lost the war. My happiest and most joyful memory was to see this arrogant and cruel army vanquished and completely routed.

I then became a free man and there wasn't any need to remain under cover any more. I was called back into the army in January 1945 and I took part in the fight of the Atlantic Pocket. After May 8th, I was sent to North Africa and was demobilised in June 1947.

*The Germans rounded up all the villagers. The men were taken to nearby stables where they were shot. The women were taken to the church. The German soldiers then locked all the doors and set fire to the church. The women were burnt alive. However, not everyone died. One of the mothers threw her newly born baby through the church window and he survived. Moreover, a couple of children who were playing truant from school were in the fields when the tragedy happened. They then locked all the doors and burnt the church down. The village to this day is kept in ruins as a poignant reminder of the evil of Nazism.

The most memorable moment of this war is my escape from the concentration camp and the victory parade on The 8th May 1945 in Orleans.

Regarding the war, I would like to tell young people, honestly and truthfully, without any bias, what my life was like and the life of the people who experienced this war. The hardship, the deaths. Between 10th May 1940 – 25th June 1940, 200,000 French soldiers were killed. (Nearly 2 million were made prisoners.) The deportations, the ruins, the destruction, the invalids, the atrocities caused by the Germans.

I would tell them to think long and deep about all this. To think about all those that are dead and all those that suffered, so that you are free and that you live in peace. Today with the European Union and the Treaty of Friendship between France and Germany, it is said that we have to forgive, but I find this too difficult to do. For you perhaps it is different, but be vigilant, peace is fragile but shout loudly, "Never again the war and don't forget all that happened between 1939 and 1945."

Lucien Baudon was only eight years of age when the war came to France. His story is seen through the eyes of a child. Whilst children in England played in craters and collected shrapnel for souvenirs, Lucien experienced at first hand life under the Nazis. Lucien is Valerie Baudon's father.

Lucien Baudon.

I was born in 1931 and I lived with my parents in a small town in the countryside, located 3 kilometres from the Loire and 15 kilometres from 'Chateau de Chambord," which is the most beautiful castle in France. As I was only eight years of age at that time, I couldn't understand the events but like every kid, I was a very curious being.

When I was at home I often hung from the iron gates of the yard to see the soldiers in their uniforms passing who sang and marched in time towards the practice ground, situated one kilometre from our home.

This obviously made me nervous and to add to this my mum had already experienced the German occupation at the Belgium border, during the First World War.

In June 1940, various radio programmes were sending out propaganda saying that the Germans would not cross the Loire as the French army would set up a defence line on the Loire, similar to the one in 1916. As we were living by the side of the river, my father decided to take my mum and myself to my grandmother's, one hundred kilometres south of the resistance zone. It took us such a long time to complete that journey by car, more than a day I think. The road was congested with elderly people, women and children who were walking, on bikes and in carts. They were loaded with their belongings and running away from the North of France and the Paris area.

On the verges of the road were some columns of French tanks whose crews were waiting for the arrival of the Germans with dismayed faces. They were stranded due to the lack of fuel and ammunition. And I remember that my father grumbled and swore that we would lose the war in less than a fortnight. Indeed, my father came back to fetch us, by car, on the arranged day. The way back was also congested with civilians and carts, which were coming back up to where they had started. Some German soldiers with helmets and guns were moving the people on at every crossroad. I have never forgotten this part of my life.

During the afternoons in the school holidays, I used to go for a walk in the fields and there were many times when I met German soldiers on manoeuvres. Running around me, lying on the ground, jumping and shooting in the air. I used to carry on walking impassively, watching them, watching them making all this fuss. They never said anything to me and never forbade me to walk through the field. Sometimes they smiled at me, I didn't bother them. My mother always panicked when I went there.

The dressmaker used to call at my house for me to try on a pair of trousers or a jacket or overcoat, that she had tailored from an old suit, whose fabric was faded by the years and hadn't yet been moth eaten. Also, when my parents took me out to buy a new pair of ankle high shoes with a voucher, distributed by the town hall. The sole was in white wood. On our return from the shops, my dad hurried to shoe them, because I easily wore them out and these pair of shoes had to last the longest time possible.

The saddest memory for me during the war was when Mum became ill in the winter of 1941. It was on a Sunday, there was a lot of snow and it lasted a long time. However, my dad still sent me to school. I was often cold and to this day I still hate the cold.

One day in the summer of 1943, I was gleaning some ears of corn for our three hens, when suddenly, two Mosquito planes with striped wings suddenly appeared hedge hopping. They flew two big circles around me. Understanding what was probably their signal, I rushed to a ploughed field where I sprawled myself in a large furrow. As soon as I was lying down the two fighters started to machine-gun a locomotive that had stopped in the station. The cartridges fell all around me, as I was only a few hundred meters away from their target. When the machine-gunning was over, the Mosquitoes passed above my head and made again two arcs, maybe to thank me for not hindering their mission. As I got up after they had completed their first circle, I waved goodbye to them. When I arrived home with my pockets full of cartridges still hot, I found my mum in tears for she knew where I had been. Nevertheless it did not prevent her from giving me a very stiff thrashing. As far as I was concerned, I was proud of my involvement.

The happiest day was when three American N.C.O's came to my home to give me a German bicycle. I was thirteen years old and it was my very first bicycle. I painted it apple green and used it until my twentieth birthday.

In August 1944 as I was coming back from shopping one afternoon when I told Mum I had come across a jeep with four American soldiers. One of them stretched his arm out and made the victory sign to me. Of course my mum did not believe a word of my story. Therefore she was very surprised when two or three hours after my account, a big column of American tanks travelled through the country. The soldiers sitting on their tanks threw some small parcels to us; in which we found powdered milk, coffee, soup, potatoes, and eggs for the first time.

When my dad arrived home that evening, he hurried down the cellar to fetch a bottle of sparkling wine, which had been hidden in the sand in a dark corner. This was probably the first time I had a hangover.

This is what I would say to a young person about the war.

I would like to make him/her understand that the war is the biggest human folly that can exist. I would tell him/her that he/she should not play with any toy guns.

Also bombs and nuclear weapons do not choose their victims. They disfigure, kill, cause deformities, destroy wealth, and impoverish populations bringing to every home sadness, irreparable despair and rancour. It is very difficult for the victims of such a tragedy to forgive.

The ideal world would be for all nations to live in peace. Hence, the importance of developing international exchanges between young people. Sporting competitions, pilgrimages, such youth meetings in Rome and Jerusalem, tourism, work experience abroad and the Internet can also help bring peace.

In case of foreign invasion or occupation you shouldn't think of fleeing your country. On the contrary it is better to chase away all the negative thoughts in your mind. One must find the courage, the will to fight, to defend one's family, country and freedom. Never admit defeat! Even if it means sacrificing one's own life to serve the values of liberty.

We have heard stories of the devastating effect the Blitz had on Birmingham and Coventry. Clare Hayes, who hails from Ireland, remembers the V1 and V2's, that fell on London late on in the war. They were called Vergeltungswaffen, or revenge bombs. The first V1 to hit London was in June 1944. They were to prove to be devastating and Hitler although losing the war on mainland Europe was not going to give up that easily as he sought revenge!

Clare Hayes of Erdington.

I spent the war years in London. I had come over from county Galway and came to live with my sister Bridie in Hounslow.

During the 1940 and 1941 the bombing of the city was most severe but no worse than Birmingham and Coventry. During 1942 the bombing became less severe. We still had air raid warnings even when we were in the cinema and watching a very interesting film. The alert was flashed on the screen and the location of the various shelters was given but few people bothered to leave and carried on watching the film!

For war work I had the choice of joining the forces, working in a factory or work on the buses. I chose the buses. I lived in a flat on Hounslow High

Street. When the German planes came over there was a constant movement of gun carriages on the High Street especially during the night. After the war we noticed the walls of the flat were very badly cracked.

When Hitler decided to invade with the V-1 and later V-2 bombs, that for me was the most worrying time. The V-1 otherwise called, 'Doodlebugs' were terrifying. They made the most awful noise and when the clouds were low, it was very difficult to decide if the bomb was to fall quite close or far off. They looked like small planes but had no pilot and they had a fire in their tail, like calor gas and Bunsen burners. When the fire went out the engine stopped and the 'plane' glided down. The explosion was terrific. The bomb didn't make a crater but shattered everyone and everything in its path. During that period the public were asked to use the public air raid shelters and this meant going down every night with a blanket and pillow. The wardens took everyone's name and address so that in the case of houses being destroyed they would have a good idea of who was missing, if any.

If I was on an early run on the bus it meant that I had to leave the shelter by 4.00.a.m. The first bus left the garage at 5.a.m. On the way back to my flat I used to be so frightened as they were coming over in droves. As I mentioned above, when the cloud was low it was very hard to make out where they were going to fall. One heard the engine stop and then silence. The silence lasted for about fifteen seconds and then the sound of the explosion. During those fifteen seconds you did not know if you were going to live or die. However, although it seemed near it could have gone off a few miles away. I think it was the uncertainty that made one frightened. I was more times lying down on the street with my pillow and blanket than I care to remember. When I did reach the flat and put the kettle on I found that I was racing down the stairs so many times because I could hear them coming over. Then on the way to the garage I was frightened of the shop windows blowing out. I would walk down the street and my heart was banging away!

One evening, a crowd of us was going out to a hotel, which was in Osterly Park. My sister, Bridie, decided that we should cross over the road as she had some letters to post. Lucky for us because just as we crossed the road one of the Doodlebugs came right over Barclays bank, which had very large chimneys. I was so sure that it was going to hit the chimneys. The flying bomb's fire went out and the engine stopped. We all knew what would happen next so on the ground we went. It glided right over the Red Lion Hotel and onto the Underground embankment. The explosion was so loud. I had a splitting headache for days afterwards. All the houses adjacent to the railway line were shattered and a number of people had been killed. We were lucky to have crossed the street when we did as all the windows on that sides were blown out. The glass could have cut us to ribbons. There were clothes, shoes, and even bread blown out from the shops and lying on the street. I remember seeing all the windows of the flats blown out and the curtains fluttering in the breeze. At the time of the bomb the workers were coming home from work. When they heard the V-1 cut its engines they all jumped off their bikes and threw themselves on the ground.

The Doodlebugs didn't hit Hounslow as badly as the City. It seems that they were not powerful enough to travel very long distances and some of them were intercepted by fighter planes and guns when they came over the coast. It was just as well that they did as the barrage balloons were no deterrent, and as the flying bombs travelled so fast it was difficult for the searchlights to hold them in their beam. With the V-1 rockets one had an idea of where they were because of the loud buzzing noise but it was totally different with the V-2's or rockets as they were called. When they came over they were silent, not a sound could be heard until they reached the target. As the explosion was large they left a huge crater. The sound of them was like a strong breeze or sigh in the wind. It felt quite strange.

One evening about six o'clock the driver, Sid Ware and I had finished work and we were in the garage and I was directing him to put the bus on the stand for the night. I was standing on the platform guiding him in when suddenly my tummy seemed to roll over. It was a horrible experience and we found out later that a V-2 had come down about three miles away. It landed on a field and made a huge crater but no one was killed or injured.

On another occasion, while out on the road with the bus I heard the sound of the dreaded Doodlebugs. Again with the low cloud I was not sure how close it was so taking no chances I got the passengers off the bus and into a field. The thing went off but fortunately it was quite some distance away. However, we could see the cloud of smoke. I heard that a bus got a direct hit from a Doodlebug. There were no passengers on the bus at the time but the driver and conductress were killed outright. So devastating was the explosion all that remained was the conductress's badly damaged ticket rack!

Churchill warned us of, "Pilotless planes" but at the time people thought he was slightly mad. His words soon proved to be true and I remember a V-2 had a direct hit on a factory on the Great West Road and killed most of the night shift.

I remember watching all the RAF bombers flying out from Heston Airport. They used to leave in the evening. They all flew out in formation but when they returned they came home in ones and twos. Some would drop blue flares to indicate that there were wounded on board. I thought it was so sad for the ones who did not return.

I also thought about my husband, Patrick Hayes. He was a Chief Petty Officer in the Royal Navy and was more than often abroad. He had been on the HMS Ajax and was at the Battle of the River Plate. He was also at Dunkirk and Normandy. I never knew where he was as he wasn't allowed to tell me.

Another time we were told that the Germans might invade. The Air Raid Wardens had their First Aid post on the side of the roads. They always hung a sign outside indicating **ALL CLEAR or ALERT**. Once, for three whole days the ALERT sign was to be seen. We wondered but of course we weren't told a thing but something was going on for sure.

So many people died the young men in the Forces, the people in the bombing. One wonders if it was all worth it. What would they say if they could come back and see the state of things now?

On V.E. Day we decided to go down to the hotel in the park. There was a large crowd of us all merry and bright. I wondered as were sitting there with our drinks where my husband, Pat, was. Although crowded I looked towards the door of the lounge where we were sitting and there he was, in his Royal Navy uniform, walking through the doors of the Osterly Hotel! The feeling I had was just great! He was in the navy and I had no idea where his ship was. I really didn't expect to see him but as it happened his ship was in Scotland and they were moved down to Chatham in Kent.

There are so many things that happened during the war and it would take an age to write them all down. However, I think I have told you the most important ones.

C.P.O. PJ Hayes, husband of Clare Hayes.
C.P.O. Hayes was on the HMS Ajax at the Battle of the River Plate.
The first British and Commonwealth naval victory of the war.

Dramatic photograph of the German pocket battleship, Graf Spree, being scuttled in Montevideo harbour, December 1939.

Lest we forget.

As a child my brothers and I had a model village in the attic of our large Edwardian house. It was supposed to be a French village. The railway station looked authentic enough with its long platforms and locomotives, however, the semi-detached model houses gave the game away! Hours and hours were spent playing with Airfix soldiers, Germans, British and American. Chunky Sherman and Churchill tanks would take on the might of Panzer and Tiger tanks. Stuka dive-bombers would carry out dogfights against Spitfires and Wellington Bombers. An "Armistice" would be called when Mom called us down for tea.

That was war played in an attic and seen through the eyes of children. I was also mesmerised by Dad's wartime stories and looked with pride on his array of medals. His photo album included picture of the Graf Spee, the German pocket battleship that was scuttled in Montevideo Harbour after the battle of the River Plate, December 1939. He also taught me about the tragedy and horror of war.

After researching WE'LL MEET AGAIN I have experienced a gamut of emotions. I have admired ordinary people's resistance and resilience. I

119

have felt humility as they told constant stories of hardship and how they got through it all.

I recoil at the waste and horror of war that took place on this wonderful and unique planet we call, Planet Earth.

As I sleep in the back bedroom of my house I think of Billy Bagnall whose bedroom it was during the war years. He was an officer n the signals serving in Baghdad. I imagine him coming home on leave, alighting at the pretty Victorian railway station. I imagine Billy walking down tree lined Wheelwright Road, kit bag slung over his shoulder. No doubt he was relieved to see his family. I think of him lying in bed wondering what his fate would be. He survived the war. He was one of the fortunate ones.

I want to end with a note of thanks, a thank you to all those that gave the ultimate sacrifice, to those that fought, defended this realm so that we can live in liberty. It is to them this book is dedicated.

In a world of faxes, mobile phones, internet and computers it is refreshing to pause for a moment outside any major hotel in the city and now see the colourful array of world flags fluttering in the breeze. Yes, we will all meet again some sunny day but let us hope as Woodrow Wilson hoped in 1918 that the "Grey Skies" would be chased away forever.

Pax Vobiscum.

Patrick B Hayes.

All Saints Eve 2000.